Wonderfully Made

What The Bible
Says About
the Human
Race

Akwasi O. Ofori

Paperback ISBN: 979-8-9904106-1-9
Hardcover ISBN: 979-8-9904106-0-2
Ebook ISBN: 979-8-9904106-2-6

Cover design by Jess LaGreca, Mayfly book design

Library of Congress Catalog Number: 2024906175
First Printing: 2024
Printed in the United States

What the Bible Says Series Book 1

Dedication

To my daughter, Adwoa, called home too soon.
I am hoping to see you at the resurrection.

Acknowledgments

My overflowing gratitude to Almighty God, who gave me insight into his scriptures.

Sincere thanks to my wife Betty and daughters Benefaa and Abena who read the manuscript and made meaningful suggestions for improvement.

Contents

Chapter 3—By Grace I am Saved

Chapter 6—I Restore Fourfold

Chapter 7—God in Christ Forgave Me

Chapter 8—He Opens My Ears by Adversity

Introduction

This little book, *Wonderfully Made*, attempts to help believers discover their position in the Lord. It looks at humanity's origins, our position in the created order, the fall, and its consequences on our relationship with God.

The fall, the phenomenon in which the first couple disobeyed God's directives, severed the relationship between humans and our creator. This book tries to show that though the fall burdened us with the responsibility to find our way back to God, he did not leave us to struggle on our own to do this.

He made provision for his son, the Savior, to come and die on the cross to be the atoning sacrifice for humans. In his death, God has provided a path to salvation for all who believe. Salvation is an act of unmerited favor shown to humanity by a loving God.

The book also looks at the relationship of humans with one another. It suggests that sometimes we commit offenses against each other. Such instances call for acknowledgment of our wrongdoings and the need to restore things we wrongfully take from others or acts we commit against each other.

It touts God's desire for reconciliation between us and other humans and God. Additionally, it investigates life after death and the fate of humanity in general when we depart our earthly bodies.

This book taps on the Holy Bible to make any point. For that reason, one can only gain an understanding by reading it with the supplement of the Bible. Consequently, at the end of the book, notes supporting the various sub-headings are provided.

For a better understanding of the book's substance, the reader is entreated to study the different topics along with the notes of Bible quotations provided.

Rev. Akwasi O. Ofori
Denver, Colorado, USA

I am Wonderfully Made

"Then God said, 'Let us make man in our image, after our likeness.
And let them have dominion over the fish of the sea and over the
birds of the heavens and over the livestock and over all the earth
and over every creeping thing that creeps on the earth.'"
Genesis 1:26

How did we get Here?

Zario Amandi emerged from a house in the neighborhood, his face haggard and wearied. He has been working in that house, caring for an aged client. Though he worked overtime most days, his bank account did not show his efforts.

He had come to America from his native South Africa, hoping to enjoy the country's riches. However, he could not find a job in his trained profession on arrival.

As a medical doctor, he was now working as a nurse's aide. He had racked up credit card debts because his wages were insufficient to care for him and his family. As he got into his car to go to his second job, he wondered out loud why he was even here on earth.

The Origins and the Fall of Humanity

To understand Zario's struggles, it would be necessary to go to the roots of how humanity came to inhabit this earth. The origin of humankind, according to the Bible, was a humble one. At the same time, our creation was quite intriguing, the masterful action of a master designer.

It was a collaborative action from the creator with a pure desire to fashion subject-servants who will not only do his bidding but one who will share his glory and authority and take control of all his handiwork.

At the onset, when he began the act of creation, God said, "Let us make mankind in our image, in our likeness (Genesis 1:26)." So, clearly, the creator intended to make a person in his true resemblance. One who had the authority to rule over the fish of the sea, the birds in the sky, the livestock, and all the animals that roamed the forest.

It is quite remarkable that God had such a worthy objective when he created humankind. Interestingly, the power he gave humanity extended to control over the earth and its contents and the entire created order.

In giving people control over every seed-bearing plant on the face of the earth and every tree with fruit with seed in it, the creator was emphasizing the need for humans to maintain a continuous and abundant supply of food while conserving biodiversity.

Similarly, in yielding the control of the beasts of the earth, the birds in the sky, and the fish in the seas and rivers to humans, God was underlying the need for a balanced diet for humans to aid their development.

The masterstroke of God was that before any shrub had appeared on the earth or before any plant had sprung up, he had sent streams from the ground and watered the whole surface of the earth.

Later, God would send rain on the earth to ensure its continued sustenance. These actions, however, were not to merely maintain a meaningless cycle. Rather, they were in preparation for his crowning act of creation: humanity.

For that reason, he formed a man from the dust of the ground and breathed into his nostrils the breath of life, and the man became a living being. Following that, God had planted a garden in the east, in Eden, and there he had put the man he had formed.

To make his creation comfortable and content, God made all kinds of trees grow out of the ground, both for their aesthetic beauty and for food for humankind. He did everything just so the man could be happy and at ease. Not much was required in return for all God did for his crowning act of creation. All the master required from the devotee was loyalty and obedience.

As if to test his loyalty and obedience, God put the man in the Garden of Eden to work it, take care of it, and to eat from it. The only exception was a tree supposedly destined for knowledge of good and evil for anyone who ate from it.

The process of creation was not only fascinating but also absorbing. God had formed out of the ground the wild animals and the birds in the sky and had required the man to give names to those species. He intended to allow humanity to appreciate its worth in recognizing that the master greatly appreciated him for bestowing such a great honor.

In this exercise, the man realized that he was the only creature of his kind. Thus, one can see that God initially wanted humans to see the need for companionship. In his wisdom, the creator would not tell him what he needed but would gradually lead him to realize his vulnerability.

The beauty inherent in the creation of humanity is echoed by the Psalmist when, in awe, he exuded in praise that he was 'fearfully and wonderfully made.'

That claim underscores the awesome power of God, which he displayed in not only creating humans but also creating the supporting cast to sustain human existence.

Notwithstanding the beauty of the creation of humankind, this exquisiteness would be marred by the actions of the first humans. They disobeyed the creator, committing the first act of defiance known to creation.

This disobedience was orchestrated by the serpent, who, though one of the creatures subjected to the first humans, managed to outwit them with its craftiness. In the process, it convinced the first couple to defy the creator's laws.

Using trickery, the devil mocked that the humans believed they were restricted from any fruit-bearing tree; in doing that, it preyed on the greedy and insatiable nature of humanity that does not only look for more but also gravitate towards higher goals.

By their actions, God perceived that humans had become like God, knowing the difference between good and evil. Therefore, he banished humanity from the garden he had planted for them.

This, however, was not before he had tasked our forebears, Adam, and Eve, to assume responsibility; the former to work for the upkeep of his family and the latter to experience the pain of childbirth.

Moreover, God put a curse between the SEED of the woman and the offspring of the serpent. This is the background upon which the history of human redemption would be based.

The First Adam Vis-À-Vis the Second Adam

There is a striking similarity between the first human and Christ, albeit in different degrees. The first human would become our demise; Christ would become our savior. Adam's demise was his mutiny; Christ's rise was his obedience.

Thus, there is a clear divergence regarding our ancestor, Adam, and our savior, Christ. The incarnation of Christ handily puts him in the realm of humanity. It is, therefore, convenient to refer to him as the second Adam.

Therefore, while the first man, Adam, received life and later died, Christ, the second Adam, died to give eternal life. The first is earthly and brief; the second is heavenly and eternal. The former brought death, the latter life.

Adam's actions led to the loss of the kingdom; Christ's deeds led to the kingdom's restoration. Adam lost the kingdom when he chose to disobey God's directions. In so doing, he surrendered his and our rights to inherit the kingdom of God. Conversely, Christ became the pioneer of our faith. He defeated the devil in a triumphant procession and dealt him a fatal blow.

This made it possible for him to take over the kingdom and hand it over to God the Father after he had taken over all the devil's territory and assumed control over him and his domain.

In overcoming the dominion of the devil, Christ paved the way for humans to leave the realm of the earthly and the fleeting nature, which we inherited from our forebear Adam.

Before the coming of Christ, death had reigned over humanity, not because we were individually culpable but because we were inheritors of Adam's impiety. Correspondingly, life would be ordered through the righteousness of the one man, Jesus Christ.

In Christ, instead of condemnation, humanity will be credited righteousness and declared not guilty before the throne of God. Additionally, there will be justification and life for all who will believe.

Position of Humanity in the Created Order

Humankind is the apex of God's creation, the crowning jewel of all he brought into being. Of all God's creation, only humanity is in the image and likeness of the creator. Moreover, as the pinnacle of God's creation, only humans were entrusted with care and dominion over the rest of creation.

As fascinating as the creation by God was the heavens that declared his glory, the seas and rivers with their vast expanse, and the wild animals with their great strength, none was more highly esteemed by the creator than feeble humanity. God made humans special, compensating for the strength they lacked with an unparalleled ability to control and dominate all other creations.

Humanity has the uncanny ability to manipulate the vast universe to meet the daily needs of civilization. Other creatures may be able to communicate with one another, but only humans can describe their feelings, desires, and aspirations in expressive language.

Furthermore, only humans have been able to channel their creativity into creating things they need to make their lives as comfortable as possible.

The Design of God for Humanity

That the creator God had a firm plan for humans cannot be overstated. His ideas were reinforced by his actions and not mere words. He designed a world capable of supporting the existence of humans by not only causing plants to spring up but also creating a vast expanse of fields that would support food-yielding crops.

These, he did so that the life of humanity on earth would be pleasant and comfortable. God reserved pride of place for humanity, such that even when we sank to the lowest level in morality, his plan to destroy us did not result in total annihilation. In this direction, God sent a flood to destroy life on earth.

Nevertheless, he had preserved Noah and his family in an ark he had instructed him to build. God's actions stemmed from his desire to continue to see humanity thriving and subduing the earth and its creatures.

Besides, his actions were to ensure that humankind would continue to flourish and multiply. Possibly, God enjoyed the praise and adoration of humans. This is gleaned from Noah's sacrifice upon coming out of the ark.

God smelled the aroma of the sacrifice and vowed never again to curse the ground because of human frailty. In his plans to salvage humanity from its plight, God set in motion a plan for our eventual salvation with a firmly established timeline.

This plan was to culminate in the incarnation of Jesus Christ. God's quest for the salvation of humanity is responsible for the incarnation because it is only a person who embodied humanity who could die for sinful humans.

Moreover, God's designs for humanity were for our restoration here on earth and to provide for us in the next world. That intent was made clear in the incarnation of Jesus.

The incarnation story was of God who became human, lived, and subsisted with humans, giving up all his glory. That story would not only culminate in the crucifixion and death of Jesus to pave the way for humankind to find their way back to God but also to become beneficiaries of his grace.

To this end, this grace of God, together with the peace ushered in by Jesus's vicarious death, continues to abound for all people who have responded to the invitation of a divine pardon that Christ extends.

Though God has provided our salvation, he expects believers to take up the mantle to spread this good news abroad. He expects that we will carry out our work of faith and labor of love with steadfastness.

Above all, God expects us to know that we have been chosen by him through the gospel of our Lord Jesus Christ. That is the reason why we can live victorious lives as believers.

Though believers are chosen in Christ, not all live spirit-filled lives. Whilst many are spiritual, a vast majority are carnal and fleshly. We shall now look at the two types of personality traits believers display.

The Spiritual Man

The spiritual man is a person who sees himself as crucified with Christ. Such a person firmly believes their lives have no value unless they live for Christ. Consequently, they perceive life as that which no longer subsists in the flesh but in faith in the Son of God.

Furthermore, the spiritual man ascribes to the lordship and the vicarious sacrifice of Christ. His or her belief is anchored further in the fruit of the spirit. This fruit of the spirit should expressly give clear evidence of what can be achieved in a person's life.

A distinctive mark of the spiritual person is that he or she is free from indwelling sin because that person denies any leanings toward fleshly tendencies. Instead, they add a spiritual bent to all they do. That affinity frees them from condemnation, first and foremost, because they have Christ Jesus in their lives.

Furthermore, their desires are not inclined to the excessive pursuit of fleshy pleasures, but they are constantly searching for the spiritual. Likewise, the law of the spirit of life in Christ Jesus has untied them from any hold that the law of sin and death previously had. The phenomenon referred to as the law of sin and death was rendered ineffectual by the cross.

In sending his son, Jesus, in the likeness of sinful flesh, God effectively condemned sin in the flesh. The fallout from that act is that the moral demands of the law are now met instinctively in the spiritual person. Now, their desire is not the fulfillment of the law's requirement, but that of genuinely seeking to promote the things of God.

Arguably, those who live according to the flesh set their minds on the things of the flesh, but those who live according to the spirit, the things of the spirit. The spiritual person attains the right of adoption as a son or daughter through his or her association with Christ through the spirit. Such persons owe their new state to the vicarious work of Christ Jesus on the cross.

Therefore, they are not obligated to satisfy fleshy desires because Christ's salvation came without conditions. Moreover, since the spiritual person recognizes himself or herself as chosen by God, he or she has a compassionate heart. Moreover, such people are meek and humble in their lives, and their demeanor is cloaked in kindness, humility, and patience.

The Carnal Man

The carnal man is the exact opposite of the spiritual man. This person loathes anything associated with God. His upbringing is of a person of the world whose interest is the pursuit of vanity.

His thought pattern is not only seethed in vainglory, but he is constantly filled with unwarranted pride in himself and his achievements. Such a person's narcissistic tendencies lead him to assume that the world revolves around him. Therefore, he is under the assumption that any thought of ascribing to God greatness for his accomplishments is a blight on his successes.

The concerns of the carnal man have an otherworldly value. Thus, he is solely concerned with the world of here and now, seldom giving thought to the things of God. As such, he never contemplates how he can please God in any way. He is unable to distinguish between what pleases or displeases God.

Consequentially, the carnal person practices sinning. His actions are, therefore, within the purview of the devil. His penchant for sin is identical to Satan's, who has been sinning from the beginning and has never sought to restrain himself.

The carnal person is always giving in to impure thoughts and all the other social vices. Likewise, he does not love God or the things of God. If such a person confesses any heartfelt love of God, it is insincere and has no honesty in it. No wonder such people follow the deceits of the heart and remain disloyal to anything religiously inclined.

Unlike the Spiritual person who recognizes self as chosen by God, the carnal person makes no such claim. Therefore, his or her life pursuits are not contemplated in consideration of God's word. For that reason, they are full of pride, and their arrogance knows no limits.

Humanity and Christ

Christ, meaning "the anointed One," which is the Greek rendering of the Hebrew "Messiah," is the one promised by God after the first couple, Adam and Eve, had disobeyed his directives. The many things we see around us, or even those in the heavenly places, originated from Christ.

In Christ, the visible and invisible come together. He orchestrated the coming into being of kingdoms and dominions, the heavenly and the earthly. In him is the epitome of all that is stately and grandiose.

The incarnation of Christ was made possible because of God's desire to see humankind restored to favor. You see, in the human act of disobedience, we were to suffer death and alienation from God. However, God, in his wisdom, fashioned an escape route for humanity to flee from the consequences of sin.

For these to be possible, God sent Jesus, who Christians believe is the Savior, to take on human flesh in a process called incarnation. Thus, Jesus Christ became the facilitator in the incarnation, playing a reconciliatory and mediatorial role between God and humans. It was through his shed blood that he was able to become our compensatory intermediary to lead us back to God.

Now, the door to God is opened again by Christ to lead all who believe in him back to him. He removed humankind's hostility toward God and restored us to favor once again.

For that reason, God no longer sees us as reproachable and blameworthy. Instead, he sees us as a people who have been cleansed in the sacrificial blood of Christ.

Hence, God confers a new status on the believer so that she or he can be clothed in a new image of righteousness, free of enslavement to sin.

Naturally, the work of Christ makes it imperative that all humans recognize him as the sole intermediary between God and humans. Christ's relevance in people's lives is not simply that he took on human nature.

However, it is in the fact that by becoming flesh and blood just as humans are, he was able to experience pain and the emotions familiar to us. More importantly, he was able to live a perfect, sinless life. Therefore, he became the perfect sacrifice to save us from our sins. Likewise, his action allowed him to wrestle control over death from the devil.

Moreover, by taking on human flesh, Jesus, the Savior, became a high priest who went through the same grind we go through. His life was full of sweat as ours is full of toil.

The pains and frustrations we feel were the same that he felt. He wept just as we weep and suffered just as we do. He was tempted as we are but without sinning. Therefore, he can empathize with us in our weaknesses.

Contrarily, though Christ was tempted just like us, he never yielded to temptation and was devoid of sin. He could hold on and stay faithful to his God and Father. That is the standard he set for his followers, that we should not give in to sin in our trials and temptations. Instead, we should hold on to our faith, trusting that God will vindicate us in the long run.

Permissible Human Behavior

As regards humans, there is certain conduct that God recommends. These are not necessarily essential requirements; however, they are commendable in that they will allow us to cohabit the earth and live in peace and tranquility.

To begin with, we need to be humble in all our dealings with God and other people. Second, we should eschew all tendencies to be jealous of others' achievements and create unnecessary rivalries and conflicts.

Besides these, not only permissible but admirable behavior is to care for one another. Undoubtedly, if we help take care of each other's children and property or show hospitality to all people, particularly strangers, widows, and orphans, there will be more harmony in our world.

In a nutshell, the permissible and the proper thing to do is to care for the needy and the deprived. One should not be greedy or arrogant, whilst others cannot find pride in their existence. Neither should one crave for the world when others have next to nothing to their name.

After all, what does one gain when seeing others suffering while basking in wealth and opulence? Invariably, there is no sense in amassing wealth for oneself and watching others go hungry and homeless. Neither is there any meaning in clamoring for material possessions whilst others wallow in abject poverty and distress.

Rather, the sensible thing to do is to recognize that in seeking to move up in life, one does not trample on others. Rather, always seek never to pass the chance to show kindness and empathize with those in their time of need.

Forbidden Human Behavior

Much as God permits certain behavior from us, there are things he abhors and strictly forbids humans to indulge in. Prominent on this list is any form of sexual behavior that seeks to debase our common humanity. God, our creator, expects us to have normal sexual relations with other humans. For that reason, the only accepted form of sexual intercourse is that between a man and a woman.

Likewise, murder or any form of violence or molestation is detestable by God since it destroys the image of God in us. This will include any form of oppression against a person or groups of people.

Furthermore, any show of partiality or divisiveness is abhorred by God because, in the mind of God, all humans are created in his image. This will rule out any form of hatred or the expression of hostility towards other people. Instead of rancor and anger towards one another, God expects all humans to live in peace.

Humanity and Divine Providence

God has always provided for the needs of humans, be it food, water, or shelter. He takes care of humans just as he cares for the birds in the sky or the numerous wild animals that roam the face of our earth.

God's providence goes beyond the provision of these basic needs. The very nature of the earth, its position from the sun and the moon, the sea, the rivers, lakes, and streams that flow through the earth, ensures that human life is not only catered for but also protected.

Remember how God made garments of skin for Adam and his wife when they realized they were naked after the fall? Remember how he had told them to take care of the created order and to find their need for food from it?

What can surpass such generosity on the part of God? Humans should never be under any allusion regarding the Lord's providence and continued sustenance.

The Divine Law and the Death Penalty

Generations of people have talked about the death penalty. However, if God did not punish Cain when he killed his brother Abel but instead put a mark on him so no one would kill him, why do we, as humans, execute criminals?

Perhaps using the example of Cain to speak for or against the death penalty is difficult. His example bucks the trend because the circumstances seemed different. Cain made a special request to God, which, in his sovereignty, he decided to grant.

No matter what conclusions one comes to, it remains clear that God meant for human life to be sacred, esteemed, and treasured. No individual has a right to take the life of another. The ideal situation is that no one will seek the ill of a fellow human, and we will all live in peace.

However, there are and will always be people prone to evil. For that reason, as humans, we have clear directives for what is good and appropriate behavior. In this direction, there are clear guidelines in the Holy Scriptures for those entrusted with our safety to follow.

Therefore, provisions should be made for those who take others' lives. Those were supposed to pay with their own life. God required accountability not just from humans but also from animals. He wanted us to be held responsible for our actions.

He authorized humans to put to death any person who took the life of another. "Whoever strikes a man so that he dies shall be put to death" (Exodus 21:12), God instructed.

Hence, it is safe to say that the death penalty is not the invention of humans. It is the wish of God that those in authority carry out such extreme punishment to serve as a deterrent to people who will otherwise put no value on human life.

In his letter to the Romans, the apostle Paul asked believers to be subject to those put in authority to govern them. He claimed that all governments were from God. Therefore, those in authority are acting as God's representatives on earth.

In asking believers to submit to governing authorities, Paul implied that they have the power, among other things, to collect taxes and execute criminals. He asserted, "If you do wrong, be afraid, for rulers do not bear the sword for no reason" (Romans 13:4).

CHAPTER 2

In Sin did my Mother Conceive Me

*"Everyone who makes a practice of sinning
also practices lawlessness; sin is lawlessness"*
1 John 3:4

Perspectives on Sin

Nine in the morning, Ryan heard a knock on his door. Since it was a Saturday morning, he was not in a hurry to get out of bed, particularly with a beautiful brunette sleeping beside him.

When the person continued to knock, he reluctantly got up and headed to his door.

"What brings you here this early morning," he said to his friend Thomas, who was beaming at him in the early morning sun.

"Just checking on an old friend," Thomas replied.

Ryan invited his friend to come inside. As they talked, the brunette came into the living room wearing loose pajamas with her arms crossed over her chest.

"Oh, I didn't know you had a visitor," Thomas said, pinching the bridge of his nose.

When the brunette retreated inside, Thomas looked at his friend tersely. He did not say anything, but the silence was accusatory enough.

"What are you thinking," Ryan asked, noticing the accusation in his friend's eyes.

Thomas broke eye contact to escape the sarcastic gaze of his friend. Ryan was not married, but he was never devoid of a partner in bed if he chose. He was aware of his friend's disapproval in such situations.

"Now, tell me in plain language if you think I am a sinner," Ryan accosted his friend.

He had previously rejected Thomas's invitations to go to church with him. Surely, he was not ready to throw his lot with people who would accuse him of sin at the slightest opportunity and are also judgmental.

Ryan's case is not unique. Often, people whose lives are averse to the laws of God accuse others who point them to the truth of being judgmental. Nevertheless, scripture is plain about the fact that humanity has been separated from its creator through acts that go against the law of creation.

What is Sin?

Like Ryan, many people are unsure about what sin is and its role in humanity's everyday life. We shall, therefore, take a closer look at the subject.

Sin is described variously as missing the mark or a transgression against divine law and order. If one knows the right thing to do and fails to do it, it would be considered a sin on the part of that person.

Another way to describe sin is to say that a person blatantly disregards what is proper conduct and instead chooses to do only those things that go against the norm of accepted behavior.

Most acts that are regarded as sin usually come from within a person's innermost being. Such acts would include evil thoughts, sexual immorality, theft, murder, adultery, covetousness, wickedness, deceit, sensuality, envy, slander, pride, and foolishness, among others.

Such aberrant acts often originate with a thought pattern and blossom into spiraling behavior that becomes uncontrollable. There are two types of sin described in the Bible: the one that does not lead to death and that which leads to death.

Ordinarily, all humans unwarily commit sinful acts. Those are promptly forgiven if we acknowledge, confess, and ask for forgiveness. Conversely, those are not forgiven if one blasphemes against the Holy Spirit of God or willfully commits a wrongful act.

Who is a Sinner?

No human can be pure because we originated from sin. It is commonly believed that each living human was conceived in sin. If that is the case, then no soul living can claim to be without sin. The Bible is emphatic in its claim that all humans have sinned.

This label means that no human is immune from sin. Each of us is prone to sinful acts, and our ineptitude constantly impedes us. This means that there is no virtue in us because our actions constantly peg us back.

So festooned are we in uncleanliness that sin often cancels our best intentions. Nothing can absolve humanity from sin, so any attempt to achieve the same would be cloaked in the highest deception. Some people have an affinity for sin. Such people openly boast about their wicked deeds and glory in them.

Any person who harbors resentment against another person is living in sin, and so is the person who plans for the downfall of others. Any person who has not surrendered their life to Christ still lives and ultimately will die in their sins.

Such people follow their sensual instincts and do what gratifies their longings. They never care to find out what it is God wants them to do with their lives; instead, they are always looking for pleasure and things that will widen the gulf between them and God.

When a person accepts Christ as Lord and Savior, that person ought to separate himself from a lifestyle of deliberate sin. If somebody claims to be a believer and still holds on to their previous lifestyle of pleasure and unnecessary merrymaking, they are still living in the world of the unbeliever. Furthermore, such so-called believers reject the power in Christ's salvific work.

What Causes Sin?

If you look at the way humans fell to the intrigues of the devil, it suggests how humans ought to watch out for the enemy and his trickery. Though the serpent was able to use its craftiness to outwit Eve, the desire on the part of Eve and later Adam to be like God made it easier for his plans to succeed.

Thus, when we do not accept our state in life, we become likely candidates for deception. Like how Eve fell, humans coming after Eve have always fallen into sin when lured by insatiable desires. Understandably, the desire for fame, success, or pleasure can trap the unguarded person to fall prey to the intrigues of the evil one.

Often, our desire for the pleasures of the world entices us to become victims of the devil's maneuverings. Besides, prevailing trends dictate our desires and drive us toward sin. These days, people are more self-centered and have a great affinity for worldly pleasures.

Perhaps our insatiable desire to accumulate wealth drives us towards sin. Perhaps pride and arrogance lead us to crave more stuff and abuse others while striving for earthly gains.

It is not only adults who demonstrate callousness in their behavior. Children do not fare better. They often disrespect their parents and are generally rude to other adults. The core of society is rotten, and heartlessness fills entire communities.

Isn't it strange that those people who are often involved in the mayhem sweeping our world today are mostly young? Society seems to be losing its grip on its youth. Even those who appear to be good are only so in appearance, but hatred, cynicism, and disrespect for authority are within their hearts.

These prevailing trends pose big challenges to believers because if we fall in line, we will easily fall prey to sin. As believers, we ought to be watchful and mindful so that we do not blindly follow what is usual and acceptable to the general populace.

We should watch our lives and the friends we choose because they can drag us into the errant ways of the world. Moreover, we should watch our thought patterns because these can all drift us into sin.

The Incentive to Sin

Human desire always gravitates towards sin, which can be beyond anything anyone can imagine. Particularly in the days we live in, people have seemingly become anti-God and prone to offend God both in the way we live and what we desire.

Our sole concern is how to fulfill our fleshly desires. For that reason, we often push the things of God to the back burner. This state of mind and way of living settles for degraded lifestyles: lives that may not necessarily seek to be anti-God, but which glaringly ignore the things of God.

There is a great incentive to indulge in sinful acts. Often, we are willing to do and be anything if it will please us. We are willing to embrace any lifestyle, whether it pleases God. That kind of attitude leads to a debased lifestyle.

So, though we may not directly seek to offend God, we do not seek to obey him either. Our attitudes make us enemies of the cross in how much we spend time gratifying the flesh's desires.

The Incentive of Sinlessness

There are several incentives to a life devoid of sin. Whilst sinfulness leads to death, sinlessness leads to prosperity. If one's life is free from sin, that person is not afraid to take any step because their conscience does not work against them in any way.

The believer whose life is not dogged by sin can easily fellowship with other believers without fear. As believers, we are God's representatives, and our bodies, rightfully, can be described as temples of the Holy Spirit within us.

In our purity, we recognize that our redemption came at a great price, at the expense of Christ. Those who are blameless in their way are primed for the blessings of God.

Interestingly, our good deeds are not hidden from God. He knows those and thus rewards them accordingly. Several lifestyles compromise who we are. When we are involved in such lifestyles, we open ourselves to blackmail and intimidation.

The Consequences of Sin

Any person who is involved in a sinful lifestyle ought to watch out because no one can keep wrongs in the closet forever; eventually, they will be exposed. God is a righteous and holy God. As a result, anything which is impure cannot co-habit with him. One such element that limits a meaningful relationship with God is sin.

It limits what God can do in any person's life. The consequences of sin can be brutal. In this world, it could curtail what somebody can do. Because if you are living a sinful life, it blights your way and makes you vulnerable to attacks on your person.

The worst consequence is in the next world, where the fate of the unrepentant sinner is death and separation from God. As humans, we are all destined to die. That kind of death involves just the body, but the death caused by sin brings separation between the person's soul and God.

When angels sinned, God cast them into hell and put them in chains. The fate of the person who dies in their sins will not be any different. All sin will be punished unless a person repents whilst they are still alive.

Unrepentant sinners would be kept outside the gates of heaven along with all people who, in their lifetime, lived a life controlled by sinful acts. These people would be dealt with by God according to their uncleanness and their transgressions.

For that reason, we should always be mindful that our actions and their corresponding rewards would be similar. We cannot continue to live a life of rebellion and expect to be rewarded with peace and bliss after our lives here on earth.

The Key to the Forgiveness of Sin

Since we all are sinners because of Adam's sin, we cannot claim to be righteous because of our lifestyle. The reason is that none of us, on our own accord, can be declared righteous.

Hence, the key to the forgiveness of sin begins with the sinner's acceptance. It is only when one accepts their guilt that they can go on to ask God for forgiveness. It is appropriate that we always ask

God to regenerate us, both in our thought patterns and how we live our life generally.

Likewise, it is not enough to just acknowledge your sins. Acceptance should be followed by confession and the willingness to forsake those sins to rightfully receive forgiveness.

The perfect example we have is of King David when the prophet Nathan confronted him with his misdemeanor after his run-in with Bathsheba. In that instant, he genuinely repented and asked for God's mercy.

You see, such was the love of God for the world that he sacrificed his only son, in whom there was no guilt, so that we, through him, would have forgiveness. That action on God's part shows that he is unwilling to hold anything against those who sincerely repent from their sins.

For a sin to be forgiven, it ought not to be blasphemy against the Holy Spirit, nor should it be one intentionally committed. Furthermore, we ought not claim to have fellowship with God while we still have our hidden ways. Once we agree with God about our situation, our sins, no matter how big, are forgiven.

How to Overcome Sin

There is the still small voice, our inner mind, or the subconscious that prompts us any time we are tempted to do something against a laid down order. Often, we succumb to sin when we fail to listen to these inner promptings.

There is no better way to overcome sin than to make up one's mind to walk by the Spirit, as this will help one not to indulge fleshly desires. As parents discipline their erring children, God also disciplines believers when they sin.

If we willingly accept that discipline, it sets us on course to live sinless lives. Also, temptation comes on the unguarded person, therefore, each believer ought to be aware of his or her surroundings so that they do not fall into temptation.

Furthermore, if we continually rely on the Lord, he gives us the strength to prevail when tempted. Moreover, we ought to put up resistance to the schemes and intrigues of the devil. Another way to overcome sin is to rid one's life of any form of resentment for a fellow human.

Sin can become a habit so that the believer might become comfortable living an unguarded life. Contrarily believers should always strive to live guarded lives and a burning desire to draw closer to God.

That means we should shun sin in our lives. Otherwise, if we sin, we will be akin to the devil who has been sinning from the beginning of time.

As believers, we have the wherewithal to withstand sin because Christ's work on the cross paved the way for us to keep from sin. We can avoid sin in our lives if we learn to control our desires. We should always think of the right thoughts and involve ourselves in the right acts.

What Happens When our Sins are Forgiven?

If a person invites Christ into their lives, everything about them becomes new. Their life and way of being and their thinking and actions are directed by him. No more do they live to please themselves now their concern is for God and the things about him.

Once our sins are forgiven, we, through faith, are justified. That justification brings us closer to God and gives us exceptional peace and hope. The Savior Jesus Christ guarantees this new state of tranquility.

Furthermore, the work of Christ grants us access to the presence of God. That access we gain continually lavishes us with God's abundant grace offerings. Like how humanity became engrossed in sin because of Adam's transgressions, the work of Christ did not only bring justification, but it also took away the sting of death.

As new creatures, we must strive for perfection. We must live each day expecting to improve on our acts and how best to please the Lord. The interesting thing is that if Christ took our sins in his body to the cross, it would not give us the license to live our lives any way we please. Instead, we should reward Christ's magnanimity by seeking to live right, always following the right course of action.

Moreover, we should take things a step further by extending this generosity to those who are still living in darkness by giving them the good news of Jesus Christ. We can do this in two ways: by word of mouth and through our lifestyle.

How Should the Forgiven Live?

The forgiven should strive to live their lives to please God. They should guard against seeking self-adulation and thereby turning the honor of God into shame.

As humans, we can be irritable and unpleasant under duress. Nevertheless, as forgiven people, we should always try to be on our best behavior. There is always a thin line between fraying up and keeping tempers in check. How well we keep the balance always determines our ability to keep things under control.

Furthermore, it behooves us, as forgiven people, to constantly seek to enrich ourselves with the knowledge of God. We should seek to live each day in the will of God. That way, we will resist any temptation to return to our previous lifestyles.

Moreover, we should live life as people for whom Christ won the victory through his death on the cross. Likewise, we should realize that having been raised with Christ, we are required to exhibit high moral standards.

For that reason, our desire should be for heavenly things instead of the earthly. We should learn to be honest with each other and also learn to forgive those who wrong us.

Above all, our goal in life should be fairness. We ought to learn to be impartial and accepting of one another no matter our origin, color, race, or creed.

CHAPTER 3

By Grace
I am Saved

"For he says, 'In a favorable time I listened to you,
and in a day of salvation I have helped you.' Behold, now
is the favorable time; behold, now is the day of salvation"
2 Corinthians 6:2

The Plan of Salvation

In the previous chapter, we met Ryan, who thought his friend Thomas was judgmental for assumingly accusing him of sin. It is not only people like Ryan who sometimes presume others are accusing them of sin. We all sometimes feel that way. However, the good news is that God has a plan of salvation for us.

God's plan of salvation was hatched in the Garden of Eden after the fall of our forebears, Adam and Eve. This plan is found in the indictment of the serpent.

In this charge, God spoke specifically about the state that the serpent will assume. He specified that because of the deception of the reptile, it was cursed above all livestock and wild animals.

Further punishment for the serpent's trickery had to do with the banishment of limbs and the ability to walk like all other creatures.

Instead, its lot was to crawl on its belly and eat dust throughout its lifespan.

Moreover, God promised to put enmity between it and the woman and between its offspring and hers. Embedded in these pronouncements was the promise of a savior for humanity in the future seed of the woman who was to deal a fatal blow to the devil and its intrigues by crushing its head.

Interestingly, all the serpents would be capable of doing would be to strike the heel of the seed of the woman. On that day, God put a curse on the serpent and told him that he had a plan for the SEED of the woman to crush his head.

So, in the garden, God devised a plan for Christ's incarnation to become the world's savior. What those statements of God meant was that notwithstanding the first couple's disobedience, he was still caring.

He continued to display his love for our forebears and, by extension, all people insomuch that he began preparations for our redemption. Notice that this action of God did not take into consideration human ineptitude.

Rather, as a show of his sincerity for the eventual redemption of humanity for our sinfulness, he already set in place a process to eventually atone for our impiety with the promise of a seed who would become the world's savior.

This plan of salvation God designed was not for a selected group of people but for people of different races, creeds, and faiths. The only requirement was for the individual to accept the message of God's promised savior.

Since this promised salvation is not simply for specific people, Jews, or Gentiles, it is a cause for rejoicing for all people. As a human, you also are included in this plan of salvation. You are equally appointed to receive eternal life.

The only caveat is to believe the message of God's Son, who also serves as the messenger of this divine missive. This message, which all people ought to accept and echo, is that God, the creator of humanity, has not destined us for wrath. Instead, his fervent desire is that all people will obtain salvation through his Son, Jesus Christ, who has also become our Lord.

All have Sinned

The Bible is plain in its claim that no one is righteous before God. In the eyes of the creator, we have all sinned and have thus fallen short of his glory. Sin has tainted the entire human race.

As humans, we may strive to do good deeds. However, such efforts, at best, yield little fruit. These assumed 'good deeds' are comparable to dirty apparel.

Salvation is by Grace

Therefore, whether we were religious or not, Jewish, or non-Jewish, we were each dead in our wrongdoings and were without any hope of redemption.

That sinful nature exposed us to the devil and made us unworthy to come before God. Thus, we became easy prey for the devil who weirdly ruled over us because we lived in disobedience.

In the case of Jews, however, because of the covenant of the promise God made to Abraham, they had the better covenant promise of being reconciled with God.

Now, however, with the death of Christ, the entire human race is availed of God's promise of redemption. Jesus became our peace by making both groups one by destroying the barrier, which was the dividing wall of hostility.

He achieved this by setting aside in his flesh the law with its commands and regulations to create in himself one new humanity.

Through the cross, the reconciliation of both Jews and non-Jews was accomplished.

When God raised Jesus from death, he not only brought us back to life, but he gave us new life. This means that Jesus' work on the cross gave humanity enormous benefits.

These benefits are open to the entire human race. To become the beneficiary of this noble work of Christ is only possible through faith in Christ and not personal works.

Salvation through faith and not work became a contentious issue in the early church and was clarified only in a council of elders meeting held in Jerusalem. So, salvation by grace is now universally acceptable to Christians.

Nevertheless, being saved by grace does not give us the license to continue in a sinful lifestyle. Instead, it gives us the impetus to live our lives as people over whom sin has no control.

Salvation was Initiated by God

The need for the salvation of humanity was initiated by God himself. After the first couple broke his law, though they were separated from him, he still loved them.

Therefore, he promised to send his son into the world to save humanity from falling into the abyss. He refused to allow humans to drift away. Instead, he chose us even before the foundation of the world to make us holy and blameless before him.

The choice is not limited to a few people but to all who believe in the work of Christ on the cross. When we believe, God continues to do his good work in us until the return of our Lord Jesus Christ.

The Path to Salvation

The Bible has a clear and laid down path to salvation. This path must be traced precisely to make it easier for the believer and the seeker to find their way.

All have Sinned

The Bible clearly states that every human has sinned, and none is ever deemed righteous on their merit, not on our deeds or our religiosity. This means that we are all in need of salvation. Fortunately, the Bible outlines the steps necessary for each of us to receive salvation.

The path to salvation follows specific steps that anyone desirous of a relationship with God follows.

Repentance

The first step is repentance. It means a genuine show of remorse and a desire to put things right. In repentance, one seeks to right past wrongs and clean his or her life of any despicable acts.

Repentance became more necessary, especially after Jesus died on the cross for humanity. It ushered in a time of knowledge between what is right and wrong. For that reason, God no longer overlooks the sins of humanity. Instead, he requires people everywhere to repent.

Once a person repents, the process of forgiveness begins. Their sins are thus blotted out and no longer remembered.

Repentance means to rid one's life of all crudeness and the desire to gravitate towards sin. The repentant person embraces a life of holiness and righteous living. Their old state is replaced with the meekness that comes from imbibing the living word of God, which can give one a newness of heart.

Belief

The next step after one repents is to believe. It is a gift of God that he made available to the entire world. Our belief hinges on the God who, out of love, allowed his only son to die on the cross to give humanity eternal life.

When one believes, that belief is made manifest by the believer's actions, both before they ask Christ to come into their life and after they do so.

Note that believing is not just saying with your lips but doing that which conforms with the will of God. Your actions should not stem from seeing God in the physical sense but from trusting him for what the Bible says about him.

Confession

Confession is saying out loud that Jesus is Lord and that he died and was raised from the dead. It also acknowledges that Christ's death became necessary for humanity to have life again.

True confession is not only the words one speaks, but it is an inward belief and acceptance of the work of Jesus on the cross. Once one confesses faith in Christ, that person is justified by God as righteous.

Acceptance

The way of salvation is very narrow, and only those who genuinely confess faith are accepted.

To accept this salvation, you must recognize the power in the death and resurrection of Jesus Christ and ask him to come and dwell in your heart.

Salvation is Only Through Jesus

Salvation cannot be found in anyone else but Jesus. His is the only name through which we can be saved. He is the door anyone enters to escape the wrath of God. He is the resurrection, the truth, the source of all life, and the only way to God.

A tree and its branches typify our relationship with Christ. We can only thrive if we are constantly aligned with him, just as a tree branch blossoms when it remains part of the tree.

Just remember, once anyone accepts Christ as their Lord and Savior, they receive eternal life. He is the one who bore the sins of all humanity in his body on the tree so that humanity might die to sin and live for righteousness.

Above all, he has promised those who believe in him that no one can snatch them from his grips.

The State of the New Believer

The salvation of the believer translates them from a state of sin to that of righteousness. The word of God clearly says that when one believes in Christ, that person becomes a new being.

They earn the right to be called sons and daughters of God. Not only do they not come into judgment, but they receive the gift of eternal life in Christ Jesus.

Additionally, they have also passed from death to life. Moreover, they are sealed with the Holy Spirit, ensuring that nothing in all creation will be able to separate them from the love of God revealed in Christ Jesus.

Purpose of Salvation

God's Purpose is to Give Us Eternal Life

God's number one purpose for humanity is to give us eternal life as a token of his love. That plan was hatched in the Garden of Eden immediately after our forebears disobeyed his directions.

God's Purpose for Salvation Includes the Discipling of New Believers

Accepting Christ as one's savior and Lord is not an end. In line with the will of God, new believers ought to be taught so that they would continue to grow in their faith.

His Purpose is Always to Keep Us Safe

God saved us not because we were good or deserving. It was an unmerited favor that he made available to humanity. Having granted us salvation, he continues to protect us with his love.

To Make Us Righteous and Holy in Christ

To underline God's love for humanity, he made the Christ who knew no sin to be sin so that in him we might become the righteousness of God. Ours was, therefore, an imputed righteousness.

The Believer's Responsibility in God's Plan of Salvation

Responsibility to Maintain the Relationship with God

The believer is responsible for maintaining a relationship with God. It is a responsibility that should be carried out daily. No one is permitted to rest on their oars because they are saved.

Responsibility to Allow the Word of God to Indwell Them

The believer is responsible for allowing the word of God to take root in them. This is done through a deliberate study of the word. Besides studying the word, one ought to give it the place it requires in one's life.

Soldier for the Gospel

Our task is to be unabashed for the Gospel. We are to do everything within our reach to ensure others hear the Gospel. It could be us going personally or sending others through our financial support. Besides this, we must keep watch over what we allow into our thinking.

Our Responsibility is to do the Will of God

No one enters the kingdom of God with vain words. We should not only profess the word, but we should be doers as well. We must always realize that we were created by God and redeemed to walk in the good works exhibited by the Lord Jesus Christ.

CHAPTER 4

I am Assured

"Praise be to the God and Father of our Lord Jesus Christ!
In his great mercy he has given us new birth into a living
hope through the resurrection of Jesus Christ from the dead,
and into an inheritance that can never perish, spoil or fade.
This inheritance is kept in heaven for you"
1 Peter 1:3-4

Eternal Security

As a child growing up, I had the privilege of encountering many evangelists. Most of them came from overseas to preach in mass open-air crusades. I vividly remember that, though I had accepted Christ as my Lord and Savior, on a couple of occasions, I had gone forward again in response to the altar calls by those evangelists.

My confusion stemmed from my lack of understanding of the Christian doctrine of eternal security. This doctrine, described simply in layman's terms, is: "Once saved forever saved."

It is a doctrine with which Christians throughout the ages have contended. Once, a questioner asked the preacher D. L. Moody whether he was worried about his salvation. To answer the person, Moody asked a question of his own.

His question was about whether Noah was saved in the ark. When the questioner replied in the affirmative, he further enquired what made him saved. "It was the ark of God," the fellow replied, "as long as he was in the ark, he was saved."

Likewise, as believers, if we remain in the Lord, our salvation is assured. Interestingly, some believers argue that the doctrine of eternal security is false, and that no believer is eternally secured by simply accepting Jesus Christ as their Lord and Savior.

That viewpoint could not be further from the truth as I experienced in my own life. My calling as a minister of the Gospel has required that I travel extensively. Once, I was returning home from Atlanta to Denver, Colorado.

When I got to Hartfield Airport in Atlanta, there was a fire outbreak, so several flights, including mine, were canceled. The next day, I returned to the airport and was placed on standby. In the waiting lounge, I sat by a young man who was also returning to Denver.

As we chatted, I found out that the flight I was trying to get on was his original flight, so he was sure of getting on board. On the other hand, I was not so sure of getting on board because I had a standby ticket.

Like the man with the confirmed ticket, so is the believer's salvation assured because of the work of Christ on the cross and the word of assurance he gave his followers.

Can one Fall from Grace?

A lot has been said against the believer's security upon the confession of faith and subsequent Christian journey. There are suggestions that the believer's security is not assured.

For such people, confirmed or standby tickets do not apply in faith. Their objection is based solely on three scriptural passages from the books of Philippians and Hebrews. These passages are Hebrews 6:4-6, Hebrews 10:26-29, and Philippians 2:12.

Many of the arguments tendered against eternal security are anchored in Philippians 2:12, where the Apostle Paul tells the Christians of Philippi to "work out your salvation with fear and trembling."

What does the phrase "work out your salvation" mean here? If the implication is that you will lose your salvation if you do not work it out, does it not negate the fact that salvation is by grace? The phrase "work out your salvation" suggests that the believer unwaveringly holds on to his or her faith.

The second passage is Hebrews 6:4-6:

> For it is impossible, in the case of those who have once been enlightened, who have tasted the heavenly gift, and have shared in the Holy Spirit, and have tasted the goodness of the word of God and the powers of the age to come, and then have fallen away, to restore them to repentance, since they are crucifying once again the Son of God to their harm and holding him up to contempt.

What that passage means precisely is unclear, but what it affirms is that the person who receives the gift of salvation ought to hold on to it by refraining from a lifestyle that is unfriendly to the will of God for his children.

The third passage is Hebrews 10:26-29:

> For if we go on sinning deliberately after receiving the knowledge of the truth, there no longer remains a sacrifice for sins but a fearful expectation of judgment and a fury of fire that will consume the adversaries. Anyone who has set aside the law of Moses dies without mercy on the evidence of two or three witnesses. How much worse punishment, do you think, will be deserved by the one who has spurned the Son of God, and has profaned the blood of the covenant by which he was sanctified, and has outraged the Spirit of grace.

This third passage suggests that the born-again believer cannot make sin a habit. It supposes that if one continues to deliberately indulge in sin, then they probably do not accept Christ as their savior and Lord.

In a nutshell, people who hold such views that a believer can fall away based on these scriptures fail to take account of the larger Bible context, which we shall consider below.

Salvation is a Gift from God

It is interesting to know that salvation sprang from the love of God for the world, which caused him to set in motion his preordained plan to give his only son as a sacrifice for sin. Christ's sacrifice paves the way for anyone who believes in him to receive the gift of eternal life.

At the same time, anyone who rejects this generous act will fail to see life. Moreover, the wrath of God remains on him or her. Hence, salvation remains an act of grace by God. Our part as humans is to receive it as a gift by faith, a gift and the calling of God, which is irrevocable.

This gift of eternal life in Christ Jesus pays for the wages of sin. If the gift is given by grace, then logically, it is no longer based on works; anything short of this negates the value of grace.

The believer, therefore, ought to take comfort in the fact that when God redeems the life of his servants, it implies that they are no longer condemned. Moreover, we should always bear in mind that God does not renege on his words under any circumstance.

The Believer is Sealed by the Holy Spirit

By the one act of disobedience from our forebears, Adam and Eve, humanity stood condemned. Conversely, the vicarious death of

Christ on the cross gave humankind justification. This was an act of grace that ensured salvation for all who believed.

When a person thus becomes saved, he or she becomes a new creation. They shirk their old nature and assume a new one. Such a person attains access to God by faith.

Likewise, they are justified by faith restoring peace between them and God. Accordingly, the believer is no longer considered a stranger in the household of God but a citizen and a saint.

The Believer Becomes an Inseparable Child of God

Any person who accepts Christ as their savior has eternal life and becomes a child of God forever. Not only will such a person not be condemned but also not be separated from God by anything, be it death or life, angels or rulers, things present, or things to come.

Neither can they be separated by powers, height, depth, or anything else in all creation. God is the one who caused us to be born again to a living hope through the resurrection of Jesus Christ from the dead. He gave us an inheritance that is not only imperishable but is also undefiled and unfading.

This benefit is kept in heaven for those who, by God's power, are being guarded through faith for salvation, ready to be revealed in the last days. God himself, in his faithfulness, sanctifies the believer completely and keeps his or her whole spirit, soul, and body blameless, awaiting the return of his son, Jesus Christ.

The Believer can no Longer Live in Sin

Scripture simply confirms that the believer needs to refrain from a life of sin. According to 1 John 3:9, "No one born of God makes a practice of sinning, for God's seed abides in him, and he cannot keep on sinning because he has been born of God."

It is difficult for a true believer to make a lifestyle of sin because Christ can save those who draw near to God through him. What this means is that the saved person makes it a practice of living day-to-day to please God.

Besides, since Christ is always making intercession for believers, we are strengthened in our resolve to overcome sin in our lives. Moreover, the believer has overcome sin in their life because the God within them is greater than all the elements in the world that will draw them towards sin.

In Galatians 5:4, Paul claims that those who depend on the law are those who fall from God's grace. Therefore, for the believer who continually depends on God, the likelihood of falling from grace does not come into play.

God Guaranteed the Eternal Security of the Believer

Nothing can cause those who entrust their lives to God to stumble. Instead, they will always be at peace with themselves and with God. Such a stance would have been laughable before the arrival of Christ in this world.

Before that time, humanity was overwhelmed by sin and its implications. However, when Christ appeared, God made us alive together with him.

Not only did God give Christ the authority over all flesh, but he also gave him the power to give eternal life to any person who believed in him. Christ's work entailed forgiving humans our trespasses through the cancellation of any record of debt that stood against us with its legal demands.

With these sinful debts out of the way, our salvation was sealed by the shed blood of Christ on the cross. Through this benevolent act, God has delivered us from the domain of darkness and transferred us to the kingdom.

Meanwhile, as we continue to live on the earth, God has pledged to firmly hold on to us to present us with no blame for the return of Christ. This is one of the promises of God that ever holds sure.

Jesus Guaranteed the Eternal Security of the Believer

Jesus by his death, redeemed us from the transgressions committed under the first covenant and became the mediator of a new covenant. Subsequently, those who are called receive the promised eternal inheritance.

This assertion was affirmed by Jesus himself when he explicitly stated in various pronouncements that he guarantees the eternal security of the believer.

First, he stated that anyone who drank the water he gave will never be thirsty again. Instead, that water, he claimed, "will become in him a spring of water welling up to eternal life."

Second, he said that he gives his sheep eternal life and "they will never perish." He was also emphatic in his claim that whoever hears his words and believes does not come into judgment but has transitioned from death to life.

The Believer is Sealed by the Holy Spirit

When a person repents and is baptized in the name of the Father, the Son, and the Holy Spirit, their sins are forgiven. This allows them to receive the gift of the Holy Spirit.

Remember, the promise of the Holy Spirit is for the believer and anybody who heeds God's call on his or her life. Furthermore, once a person believes in Christ, they are sealed with the promised Holy Spirit.

This action guarantees the believer's inheritance until they possess the kingdom. Does this imply that the believer cannot lose their salvation? The answer is an emphatic YES.

Whilst a believer's acts of omission or commission can grieve the Holy Spirit of God, by whom they have been sealed for the day of redemption, they do not lose their salvation.

Whereas believers can sin, they do not allow sin to reign in their lives. The reason is that because the Spirit of God dwells in them, they no longer live in the flesh. Therefore, they can control the power that sin has over them.

Jesus' Sacrifice was Final

The Hebrew sacrificial system, as it prevailed in the Old Testament, pales in comparison to the sacrifice of Christ. In the old covenant, the priest entered the Holy of Holies with the blood of goats and calves repeatedly to make a sacrifice for sin.

Conversely, Jesus offered a once and for all time sacrifice for sin. Moreover, he did not do so with the blood of goats and calves but through his blood.

Thus, whilst the Hebrew covenant secured a covering of sins and reprieve for the sinner, Jesus' sacrifice secured eternal redemption for those who are being sanctified.

Those Truly Saved will Remain in the Lord

Jesus' parable of the Sower is a classic example of those who superficially accept the Lord as their Savior. Persons who hastily receive the gospel do not give themselves the time and the space to consider the import of their decision.

However, when things begin to sink in, they come to terms with reality and go back to their former state. Thus, they did not accept the message.

Likewise, in his letter to the early believers, the apostle John mentioned some people who left the fold of believers. These, he asserted, did not belong to the Lord and only cursorily joined the fellowship of the true followers of Christ. Such people never look up to the Lord or what they can become in him.

Conversely, true believers hope for salvation in the Lord. They believe that they have been born again, not of perishable seed, but of imperishable, made possible by God's living and enduring word.

This new birth, they believe, bequeaths them an imperishable, undefiled, and unfading inheritance. Moreover, this inheritance is kept in heaven for them by no other person than by God the Father himself.

True believers believe that through God's power, Christ Jesus protects their salvation, which he is ready to reveal on his return. For that reason, their assurance is that their citizenship is in heaven, and from it, they await a Savior, the Lord Jesus Christ.

Furthermore, they believe Christ will transform their lowly bodies to be like his glorious body by the power that enables him to subject all things to himself.

Carnal believers, on the other hand, have no such hope. Their desire is to have their immediate needs met by the Lord. Therefore, when these expectations are not met, they stray away.

Salvation as a Life-Long Process

Whereas being saved (justified) is a one-off event in a moment of life, sanctification (becoming holy) is a life-long process. It means that once one accepts Christ as his or her savior, it does not end there.

Instead, that individual should continue to study and grow in the Lord and his likeness throughout their lives.

All these imply that the Lord will rescue the person who believes in him from every evil deed and bring them safely into his heavenly kingdom. Notably, those who receive salvation did not do so by accident.

Rather, they are called according to God's purpose and fore-knowledge. These people are predestined by God to be conformed to the image of Christ. If you are thus predestined, then it means you were not only called but were justified and eventually will be glorified.

For that reason, you should believe that if God began a good work in you, he would bring it to completion on the day of Jesus Christ's glorious return. Moreover, he will make you increase and abound in love for him and humanity.

The Believer Should Mature in Faith

The believer, after confession of faith in Christ, should continue to grow in the faith, otherwise, that person is comparable to a child of noble birth who has not yet grown to inherit his or her parents' riches.

The perfect comparison is that which Paul made in his letter to the Galatians comparing children birthed through Hagar, a slave girl, and those birthed through Sarah, a free woman.

When a believer matures in the faith, he or she gets to know the inner secrets of God, becomes free from all sorts of strange teachings, and can hold on to their faith.

Christ Can Hold on to His Saints

Rest assured that as a child of God for whom Christ's body was sacrificed on the cross, God in Christ will be faithful to his promise to keep you. The Lord knows you and has his seal on you.

Not only is he able to keep you from stumbling, but he will also present you with no blame before his presence. Christ has promised the believer that he will lose no one God has given him but will raise such a person on the last day. That is the incorruptible message we have as believers from the Lord himself.

Therefore, let us not hold on to any teaching which will seek to undermine our standing in the Lord. Nevertheless, that stance should not allow us to live our lives anyhow. Instead, it should strengthen our resolve to remain loyal to the master until he returns.

CHAPTER 5

My Redeemer Lives

"For I know that my Redeemer lives, and at the
last he will stand upon the earth"
Job 19:25

God the Initiator of Redemption

When God created humans, he planted us in the Garden of Eden because he wanted a close relationship with his creation. This close relationship was severed with the fall. This phenomenon had some significant effects on humanity.

First, it brought enmity between us and our creator. Second, it saddled us with the burden of fending for ourselves. Finally, it transferred us into the domain of darkness, where Satan reigned.

Humans became fearful of one another both in deeds and intentions. Since then, we have been at each other's heels, working hard to undermine one another's interests and well-being.

Humanity's new state displeased God greatly, so he put in motion a process whereby we could be rescued from our fallen state. This is what caused God to think about a process for the redemption of humans.

Redemption, therefore, is an action initiated by God to save humanity from the fall. He saw the opportunity for humanity's redemption in the vicarious death of his only begotten son.

In Jesus Christ, God redeemed the entire human race from the state of sin. He did this by blotting out our transgressions and transferring us to the kingdom of his son.

Furthermore, he chose us in Christ before the foundation of the world to be holy and blameless in his sight. Additionally, he predestined us for adoption as sons through Jesus Christ.

The Role of Blood in Redemption

Blood is synonymous with life. Anyone with blood flowing through him has the energy and ability to live.

Conversely, if a living organism is drained of its blood, it will become lifeless. Due to the prominence that blood plays in living things, it is expedient to use it as a form of exchange to pay a ransom for a wrong committed by another. God accepted the blood of animals because "the life of a creature is in the blood" (Leviticus 17:11).

This is the reason why, under the law of Moses, animals were offered as sacrifices. When God accepted blood as an atonement, it did not mean he was malevolent; rather, he accepted it because he knew that it was the only rightful way to right an earlier wrong.

The Difference in Blood of Animals and Christ

Even though under Mosaic law, animals could be used in atoning sacrifice, they did not offer the ideal permanent solution. Scripture attests to animal sacrifice offering only a reprieve, a covering for sins.

This was the case with the Old Testament sacrifices offered by Aaron and the priests. They repeatedly entered the Holy of Holies, a place where only the chief priest could enter, to offer sacrifices.

Nevertheless, that sacrifice had to be repeated anytime the people sinned. In contrast, when Christ offered his body on the cross, he made peace with his blood and secured eternal redemption for sinful humanity, once and for all (Hebrews 10:10).

Thus, whereas Christ's body was put forward as a permanent propitiation for sin, the blood of animals only temporarily appeased God and hence was ineffective in blotting out the peoples' many sins for all time.

Israel's Redemptive Practices Forefront Human Redemption

The story of redemption was gradually unfolded and forefronted by the history of Israel. It is, therefore, impossible to talk about redemption without considering the role of Israel.

Their ceremonial laws and the sacrificial system provide a firm foundation for the work of the eventual and ultimate redeemer, Jesus. His life and work clearly showed the foreshadowing role of Israel's redemptive practices, anticipating his work and achievements on behalf of all humanity.

In their sojourning through the desert and settlement in the Promised Land, their successes and failings underscored why humanity needed a savior.

Israel's redemption laws catered to the needs of the poor and needy, albeit crude and rudimentary. For example, in the story of Ruth, Boaz, according to Jewish law and practice, made some reservations for poorer people to benefit from his farm by leaving some grains unharvested so that the needy could help themselves. This came as a great help to Naomi and her daughter-in-law Ruth.

Moreover, their laws showed the frailty of human nature in obeying laid down rules. Time and again, they committed evil acts against each other. Whilst some of these acts were intentional, others were accidental. For that reason, God provided cities of refuge for people to run to who inadvertently committed murder.

These measures were temporal. Therefore, God, in the grand scheme of things, foresaw a situation where humanity needed salvation, not of a temporary kind, but that which would endure to benefit the eternal status of all people.

Aside from the fact that these acts and many others had temporary efficacy, they were a foreshadowing of things to come. They were the precursor of what God would later grant to humanity in offering his Son.

When Christ appeared, his ministry seemed to have taken a similar line to the role played by God in Israel's redemptive actions. They were similarly centered around the poor and less privileged in society.

When confronted about his mode of practice, he asserted that he did not come for the righteous but for those who perceived themselves to be sinners. Furthermore, to mirror the laws given to the Israelis by Moses, Jesus was slow to condemn sinners and lawbreakers.

The Redemptive Work of Christ

When God first created the world, he made a covenant with the first couple, Adam and Eve. This old covenant, however, was broken when our forebears transgressed the laws of God. This resulted in death, which was a spatial separation from God.

This situation called for a go-between to mediate between God and humans. This is where the work of Christ came into play. Through his redemptive work, Christ became the mediator of a new covenant so that those who are called may receive the promised eternal inheritance.

His work was to show how God, in his righteousness and divine forbearance, passed over our former sins. Christ's accomplishment was made possible because he is not only the image of the invisible God but is also deemed the firstborn of all creation.

In other words, all creation passed through him. His redemptive work means the redeemed no longer live for themselves but for their Savior. Furthermore, they are tasked to continue the unfinished work of Christ in reconciling the world to himself.

Christ's Work Offered Justification

The trespasses of our forebears, Adam and Eve, led to condemnation for the entire human race. Conversely, Christ was righteous and sinless and, therefore, justified all. Notwithstanding his sinlessness, God did not send him down to the earth to condemn humanity.

Instead, he was full of love and care for sinful humans. Through his righteous compassion, Christ sought after our justification. He voluntarily offered himself to be slain so that God could accept his blood as a ransom for people of all walks of life, of every race, color, and creed.

Christ's work on behalf of humankind was not contingent on anything we had done, nor did we merit it. Rather, it was the gift of God, who put Christ forward to become the propitiation for our sins through his shed blood. God, in his divine forbearance, passed over our former sins and declared us justified.

Christ's Work Offered Redemption from the Hold of the Law

The fall of Adam and Eve meant that humans were subjected to the control of the elements of the world. We were exposed to the dictates of the law and the enemy of God, who is Satan.

Some may say that God could have, with a wave of his hands, blotted out our sins. That would have demeaned the consequences of sin. It would also have been unjust because sins incur a penalty and demand retribution to satisfy the requirements of justice. And God cannot act contrary to his divine nature of perfect holiness and perfect justice.

Therefore, God waited for the appointed time to send a Redeemer. This Redeemer was his only Son, Jesus, who offered his body on the cross as a sacrificial lamb.

The sequence of his actions meant that he took the sins of the world upon himself and died an accursed death, hung upon the Cross, that we might be freed from the curse of the Law.

Earlier in the history of Israel, the Deuteronomic law stated that anyone hanged on a tree is cursed. This equally applied to the way and manner Christ died. He became a curse by being hanged on a tree and became a worthy substitute.

His substitutionary role took upon himself both the penalty and curse of sin, thus removing its sway over humanity. This paved the way to restore the relationship of humans with God by his sacrifice, both in this life and eternally.

The Human Role in Redemption

The human role in redemption is not passive. Everyone is expected to actively participate in the redemptive act of God. This participation does not imply that humans assist God in carrying out his work of redemption.

Rather, by participation, it implies that, though Christ died on the cross to save humanity, one's redemption only becomes effectual upon that individual's confession of faith. In short, it means that Christ's pardon has to be accepted to be effective.

The implication is that one ought to cherish and put a high premium on the work that Christ did on their behalf. Ultimately, one's role in God's redemptive act should be to hold unswervingly to the hope of salvation they have received.

The Lifestyle Befitting the Redeemed

Redeemed people are called to lifestyles of humility and gentleness. They pay careful attention to the way and manner they conduct their affairs. They are ever aware of the presence of God in their lives and are always attentive to the leadings of the Holy Spirit.

They do not presume on the riches of God's kindness to under-value the work of Christ on their behalf. Rather, they recognize that out of his forbearance and patience, God carved a path to lead them to repentance.

This gives him or her the desire to maintain the unity of the spirit in the bond of peace. That person recognizes the importance of other believers and the need to collaborate with them in diverse ways. They learn from the example of Christ who out of love gave his life for their deliverance.

This lesson teaches them to show the same type of love to others within the household of God. Furthermore, their lives tend to mimic God in patience, transparency and in purity. They eschew rancor and divisiveness in everything they do.

Redemption Should Lead to Christlikeness

When people accept Christ as their lord and savior, they are not deemed perfect humans who ably control sin in their lives. Conversely, for the new believer, the Christian life is one of ups and downs.

There will be days of highs and days of lows. This, however, does not mean the believer holds on to the imperfections in their life. Their goal is to attain perfection and become like Christ.

This objective is a big incentive for believers to live a life devoid of cruelty and malice. The pursuit helps them become more rounded and mature in their spiritual journey. Their renewed mindsets ensure that they are being transformed into their perfect selves daily.

No believer ever assumed they had reached perfection. Rather, they labor daily in their quest to be like Christ in all aspects of their life. Such believers know how to draw near to God daily through prayer and the study of his word.

CHAPTER 6

I Restore Fourfold

"So if you are offering your gift at the altar and there
remember that your brother has something against you, leave
your gift there before the altar and go. First be reconciled to
your brother, and then come and offer your gift"
Matthew 5:23-24

Why Restitution?

Joe was a Christian who attended church services regularly. He also did everything necessary for a child of God to grow in the faith. However, life in Ghana was tough for him. He was a personal driver for a rich man in the city of Kumasi. Though he strived to be obedient to the Lord, the struggles of life were hard to deal with.

One day, when his boss sent him to the capital, Accra, to clear some goods at the harbor, he saw the opportunity to abscond with his car. Quickly, he sold the car, bought a ticket, and left for Germany. One day, as he read his Bible, he was convicted of his sin. Now, he not only needed to ask for forgiveness from his former boss, but he also recognized that he needed to make restitution.

The concept of restitution is taught throughout the Bible. It is the idea that a person who steals something from somebody else or improperly takes something from another must return it.

The gesture shows that the culprit is genuinely sorry and sincerely seeking to make amends. One cannot truthfully be penitent and still hold on to an item they wrongfully acquired.

The Old Testament takes the subject seriously and has made various prescriptions for it. In certain sections, the directives seem so outlandish, even bizarre.

Nevertheless, on closer scrutiny, it befitted the circumstances in which the people were at the time. This suggests that whilst restitution is still required from offending parties, it should be tailored to function dynamically in a changing society.

Restitution is a U-Turn

Restitution cannot be a half-hearted act. It demands complete surrender. It even requires that it is carried out to its completion before a believer can offer sacrifice or prayer to God.

Once a believer realizes his or her sin and makes a confession, it is demanded that they make full restitution by restoring whatever it was that caused them to sin.

For example, if one should steal something from another person, it is not enough to confess their sins. They should go a step further and restore to that person what it was they deprived them of.

It even applies to our words. Perhaps if you malign a person, it is not enough to pray for forgiveness. Rather, the proper thing to do is to acknowledge your fault to the person you offended.

Restitution is Accountability

Restitution rightfully should involve accountability to support genuine repentance. Making amends is not only the responsibility of an individual but is needed to keep all parties in an issue accountable.

As Galatians 6:1 makes clear: "If anyone is caught in any transgression, you who are spiritual should restore him in a spirit of gentleness."

Thus, not only is the lawbreaker expected to account for their deed, but society is encouraged to assist them in their restoration. Restitution sometimes requires taking the difficult path of availing oneself for retribution for past acts, the ultimate form being the death penalty, where one surrenders oneself to be killed for taking another person's life.

Restitution is a Sign of Genuine Repentance

The best example of true rebirth in the Bible was depicted by the life of a man from Jericho called Zacchaeus. Zacchaeus gained a lot of wealth through his work as a chief tax collector.

In Jesus' days, tax collectors were hated by the people. Their hatred stemmed from the fact that they collected taxes for the Romans, whom the Jews loathed.

Moreover, they seemingly collected more than they were supposed to so that they could pocket portions for themselves. For that reason, they were perceived by the Jews as sinners.

When Zacchaeus met Jesus, he truly repented from his wrongdoings. He told Jesus, "Look, Lord, I give half of my goods to the poor; and if I have taken anything from anyone by false accusation, I restore fourfold." That was a sign of true repentance because he no longer wanted to keep money and things acquired through greed.

Restitution is to Ensure Fairness

As regards ensuring fairness in the act of restitution, two biblical passages come into view: Exodus 21 and Nehemiah 5. Exodus 21 prescribes the punishment for people who inflict personal injuries on others.

If anyone committed murder, kidnapped, or even attacked their parents, their fate was the death penalty. The offenses even involved animals who damaged property or killed another animal.

However, if the act of murder was committed unintentionally, the offender was to be granted a reprieve and flee to certain designated cities. These measures ensured that life and property were protected and that any act of lawlessness was punished.

On the other hand, the Nehemiah passage dealt with how the rich in society treated the poor. The poor were taking loans from the rich to support themselves. In most cases, the repayment of those loans puts strain on them.

Some had to mortgage their farmlands and houses to repay their loans or even to fulfill their tax liabilities. Nehemiah charged the rich to take off the interest they were charging to lend out money. In some cases, he called for outright debt forgiveness.

As in the Mosaic orders in Exodus, Nehemiah's measures were to ensure fairness in the society. Whenever one gives back what they have taken unlawfully from others, it ensures that neither party is taken advantage of.

For that reason, when we restore what we have taken unlawfully from others, societal balance is secured. Above all, it brings peace and a sense of oneness to both the victim and the cheater.

Restitution is to Build a Fraternity of Believers

Restitution is recommended particularly for believers. As followers of Christ, we are a close-knit fraternity. We are not expected to hold grudges amongst ourselves. Rather, we must always maintain cordial relationships.

This is only possible if we each work to ensure that nothing becomes an obstacle in our relations. Nevertheless, sometimes, our relationships can be breached. This is where restitution comes in. Good relationships are maintained when an offender acknowledges their wrongs and makes amends.

On the other hand, if the offending parties become intransigent and refuse to make amends, relationships are broken. That is the main reason why the act of restitution is necessary to appease one's wrongs and make sleeping dogs continue to lie down.

Return, and then Some

The Old Testament teaching on restitution was very clear. People were to pay for things they wrongfully took. In extreme cases where one was unable to pay for something they took from their neighbor, they were to be sold to repay their debt. In some cases, thieves were to pay double for things they stole.

Thus, in the Old Testament, just restoring a stolen item was not enough. That is the spirit of restitution. The offending party must be made to feel the weight of their misdeed by not only paying back the initial wrong but also going above and beyond to restore more than they deprived their victim.

God Reinstates the Repentant

God restores the fortunes of believers after we repent from any previous sinful state. He did that for Israel time and again when he restored them after allowing their enemies to prevail over them.

Throughout history, God has continually reinstated people who committed acts of insolence either against him or their fellow humans. Today, he continues to do that in the lives of believers, though we repeatedly flout his orders and rules.

God himself carried out the greatest act of restitution. Though he had done no wrong, he sent his son Jesus, who was blameless, to take on his body the punishment for all our sins that we deserve so that he could restore us to a righteous state. God did this so that his relationship with humans whom he created in his image could be restored.

CHAPTER 7

God in Christ Forgave Me

"Therefore, if anyone is in Christ, the new creation has come: The old has gone, the new is here! All this is from God, who reconciled us to himself through Christ and gave us the ministry of reconciliation."
2 Corinthians 5:17-18

God, the Architect of Reconciliation

There was tension in the air as Rebecca turned the corner to go into the house of her friend Adelaide. The two were inseparable friends some time ago. They did things together until, one day, she learned that her friend had been revealing her secrets to others. Once she found out, she left their friendship and shared apartment.

Years have passed since that betrayal, but Rebecca still harbored resentment for her friend until now. She has now given her life to Christ. Daily, as she studied her Bible, she recognized the need for forgiveness and reconciliation with her old friend.

The Bible's teaching on reconciliation is clear and emphatic because it is the cornerstone of the work of Christ on the cross. It shows the desire of God to reunite with sinful humanity after a long period of separation.

He thus initiated reconciliation when he offered his own Son as a sacrifice for sin. His action stemmed from his love for humanity. Thus, in Christ God reconciled the world to himself, without considering the sins of humankind.

Besides that, he entrusted us with the message of reconciliation. What God did in reconciliation is comparable to the story of the prodigal son in Luke's Gospel. In this story, the father took the initiative to welcome the son who had squandered the inheritance he gave him.

Similarly, God elected us in the Savior before the foundations of the world to be holy and blameless before him without counting our sins against us. He subsequently declared those of us who gave our lives to Christ as a new creation.

Christ Made Reconciliation a Possibility

Christ became the channel for reconciliation when he offered himself to be crucified on the tree to atone for our trespasses and guarantee our justification. His self-sacrifice led to his disgrace to provide the sacrifice that took care of our transgressions and iniquities.

Additionally, he took in his body the punishment that brought us peace, as well as bore our sorrows, and provided us healing by his stripes. As one who knew no sin, he became sin for our sakes, enabling us to be declared righteous.

Christ, the Channel of Reconciliation

Through Christ, God has reconciled the world to himself. He has considered Christ's work and has, therefore, pardoned our sins. No longer does he count them against us.

Instead, the shed blood of Christ removed any wall of hostility between humanity and God and restored peace between the two parties. This work, which Christ did on our behalf, not only created peace between us and God, but it also gave us renewed hope that the grace of God has given us access to salvation.

Since the blood of Jesus has justified us, we have been saved from the wrath of God. Accordingly, the hitherto broken relationship has been restored.

The Role of Blood in Reconciliation

Blood is very important in reconciliation because it is a substitutionary act. As a replacement action, reconciliation replaces one person's life for another.

Since the life of every creature is its blood, the initiator of reconciliation offers his blood, in this case, life, for that of the reconciled. Blood can help with reconciliation because it cleanses its objects of the stain of sin and sets them free from the dominion of darkness.

The importance of blood in reconciliation is seen in the results of Christ's work. He became the mediator of a new covenant God enacted with believers through his blood shed on the cross.

This work ensured that all those who believed received an eternal inheritance with God. The apostle Paul taught that a will is only executed if it can be proved that the one who made it is dead.

Similarly, God's covenant with humanity could not have been implemented had the blood of Jesus not been shed. When that happened, it showed that the deliverer was no longer present in the flesh because his blood had been poured.

The importance of blood was seen in the Old Testament sacrificial system, where the priest took the slain animal's blood to the holy of holies to atone for the people's sins. However, in the case of Jesus, his death permitted him to enter heaven itself to present his sacrifice on our behalf in God's presence.

Reconciliation Preferred to Sacrifice

The Lord Jesus in his teaching, clearly demonstrated that reconciliation is always preferred to sacrifice. He taught that one should always be in the mood for forgiveness when one is praying. He asserted that even at the altar of sacrifice, if one remembers a grudge, they should go back for reconciliation before returning to perform their sacrifice.

Reconciliation, therefore, portrays the altruistic nature of our calling as followers of Christ. A believer's reconciliatory posture portrays a mature and thoughtful person who looks out for their interest and those of their neighbors.

Hence, persons who are reconciled with God are noble in victory and reconciliatory in defeat. Therefore, they easily acquire the ability to surrender their lives to Christ willingly. Such persons become a spiritual powerhouse and the backbone of God's kingdom on earth.

This new standing confers on believers the title of priests and heirs in the house of God. This position is affirmed by the reconciliatory work of Christ on the cross.

Prescribed Ways to Achieve Reconciliation

It should be uppermost in our hearts to always work for peace and reconciliation because that is how the believer develops a closer association with God. The process should begin with renewed mindsets and a pursuit of transformation instead of conformity.

It is often said that it takes two to tango. Whilst this saying is true, when it comes to reconciliation, it should begin with the initiative of one person.

When two people or parties disagree, they will drift further apart unless one party decides to work for peace. Hence, it is often assumed that a true believer will take the necessary steps to make the first approach when it comes to peacemaking.

As believers, do not consider the offending party before making a move towards reconciliation. No matter who is at fault, we take the initiative, knowing that our actions or inaction will reflect on the Lord.

Furthermore, when we fail to forgive when it is within our power to do so, we yield ground to the devil. However, when we initiate reconciliation, we thwart the schemes of the enemy and bring glory to God.

We are Partakers of Reconciliation

Reconciliation is, first and foremost, the prime objective of God. For that reason, he offered his son, Jesus Christ, to reconcile the world to himself. God did not end his efforts with his initial act. Instead, he enlisted believers to be messengers of reconciliation.

As envoys of God, he daily makes his appeal through us. We are, therefore, partakers of reconciliation, called by God to take the good news message to the world.

Our mission includes, but is not limited to, comforting the grieving, and proclaiming liberty to captives. As ambassadors, we are to do and say things that will bring joy to people.

Thus, as people who work for reconciliation, believers are never fomenters of trouble nor bearers of bad news. Rather, they are ambassadors of peace, and goodwill, who always publish and promote peace.

Moreover, we treat both the weak and strong in a like manner. As partakers of reconciliation, our lifestyles should espouse the highest standard of Christian Living. We must deal swiftly with sin in our lives.

Furthermore, we should always recognize that each believer is an integral part of the body of Christ. Therefore, we should not lie to each other, nor entertain malice and other abuses amongst our members.

Divine Initiative the Standard for Reconciliation

The believer's standard bearer is God, who in Christ forgave sinful humanity our sins. He became the initiator of salvation by offering Christ to be our atoning sacrifice.

Christ was a worthy ambassador of this initiative in that even when he was subjected to abuse and death, he asked for forgiveness for his attackers. "Father, forgive them," he cried, even when they were casting lots to divide his clothing.

God always goes above and beyond to bring people together. He could destroy us when we repeatedly and wantonly disobeyed his directives. Instead, he was patient with us not because he did not want us to die in our sins.

Reconciliation Demands Selflessness

The spirit-filled believer is always eager to maintain unity and peace. To this end, they strive to preserve close-knit relationships. Perhaps it is their quest to be worthy of their calling that undergirds their humble and gentle lives.

Not only are they plain and direct in their dealings, but they also never resort to sinister plots to undermine others. Likewise, they are understanding and forbearing even with aggressors.

To this end, they assume the persona of Christ and not only work to reconcile with others but also work to see reconciliation between others. They are always guided by the dictum, "Do unto others as you wish them to do to you."

Perhaps it is their obedience to the master's directive to 'pray for those who persecute them' that gives them the big hearts to eschew jealousies and petty quarreling. It is strange then that they are joyful in other's achievements and distressed by their loss.

A person who epitomized this behavior was the biblical character Esau. Though he is seldom considered a giant of our faith, he was a perfect example of a person who worked for reconciliation.

In this quest, he displayed true selflessness in forgiving his brother Jacob who stole his birthright and paternal blessing. Esau's behavior becomes the yardstick for believers as we seek to follow Jesus' recommendation to initiate reconciliation instead.

Invariably, it is much easier to bear a grudge. Nevertheless, as a gesture to the Lord, it is best that we always strive to reconcile even with our detractors.

CHAPTER 8

He Opens My Ears by Adversity

"More than that, we rejoice in our sufferings, knowing that
suffering produces endurance, and endurance produces character,
and character produces hope, and hope does not put us to shame,
because God's love has been poured into our hearts through
the Holy Spirit who has been given to us"
Romans 5:3-5

The Age-Old Question: Why do Good People Suffer?

Zario had accepted Christ as his Lord and Savior in his native South Africa. Upon accepting Christ, he had listened to preachers who had preached that the Christian had to do well. That, however, had not been his situation.

Back home, he had lost two siblings to AIDS. Though he had been fortunate to come to America, he had not fared any better. Every day, he thought that he had wronged God in a way that was why his fortune was not improving.

Like Zario, some people deem the Christian journey as one laced with bliss and eventual success. For that reason, when they encounter mishaps in their Christian journey, they are confused beyond reason. What every believer ought to know is that our calling is not simply for blessings and miracles.

Sometimes, we endure hardships and adversities. It is, therefore, essential that we gain a clear understanding of the Bible's view on suffering.

The writer of Psalms sought answers to an age-long question from God. He marveled at the prosperity of the ungodly and wondered why, amid their sinful lifestyles, they still lived such prosperous and flamboyant lives.

The deeds of the ungodly are obvious: they hide in secret or sometimes in broad daylight to plot evil schemes against others, particularly people who are determined to live their lives to please God.

They tell lies and frame people who love God for things they have not done. They are always seething with anger when they see believers do well in any shape and size.

For that reason, they scheme to bring down the believer in any way possible. They do not mind exploiting the plight of the poor and needy for their own gain.

When they borrow, they do not repay. When they see the law catching up with them, they use every tool possible, such as bankruptcy and pretentious assets liquidation, to dodge the bullet. For all this, they still do well. On the other hand, God-fearing people can go through a lot of suffering.

As a believer, though, you should not simply seek suffering because that will be against the letter. That type of suffering will not move a needle because God does not simply want us to suffer for the sake of suffering.

As I Corinthians 13:3 alludes to: "If I give away all I have, and if I deliver up my body to be burned, but have not love, I gain nothing."

The Purpose of Suffering

Suffering, therefore, is not something believers should thirst for. However, there is a purpose for suffering. If we come to terms with that, our troubles, if they should come, will become more meaningful.

The purpose of suffering can be summed up in the words of Jesus in the reply he offered his disciples in the ninth chapter of the gospel of John. According to that text, Jesus, on a walk with his disciples, saw a man blind from birth.

As the thought was in those days, people with disabilities were seen as being punished by God for wrongdoing either by themselves or a parent.

When they saw the man, his disciples asked him, "Rabbi, who sinned, this man or his parents, that he was born blind?" Jesus answered, "It was not that this man sinned, or his parents, but that the works of God might be displayed in him."

In his answer though, while not dismissing the notion of suffering stemming out of wrongdoing, Jesus pointed them to an unusual way of thinking. He emphasized that whilst sin can generate suffering, sometimes it is to accomplish things in the life of the suffering person.

For Restoration

Suffering not only allows the believer to acquire a refined character, but it also helps them to know Christ better and experience the power of his resurrection.

Whenever we experience suffering, we share in the sufferings of Christ and become like him in his death. When the believer goes through suffering, God does not only confirm and restore them, but he also strengthens and establishes them for his eternal glory in Christ.

To Make the Believer Steadfast in Faith

The Christian life is not all coy and flush. It can be fraught with tribulations and misfortunes in our onward march to God's kingdom. If even Christ was susceptible to suffering, his followers cannot expect to be spared a similar fate.

Nevertheless, when the believer is stricken, God delivers them from their affliction and opens their ear to adversity. We see this in the life of the people of Israel during the years they spent en route to the Promised Land.

He humbled them by allowing them to go hungry and then feeding them a previously unknown food called manna. That experience showed them humans do not live by bread alone but through God's providence.

The ensuing goal of the believers suffering is to eventually reveal God's plan to them. Though suffering may be a blemish to the outer appearance of the believer, inwardly, their soul is being renewed. When we are facing hardships, it may appear painful and unbearable, but in the long run, it works out to produce the fruit of righteousness.

As a Test of Faith

Suffering sometimes comes to test the believer's faith in God. If, as a believer, one suffers for some wrongdoing, they ought to assess their lives to ascertain the reason for their trials.

However, if it is a result of being a child of God, we should take it as sharing in the suffering of Christ and correspondingly also be prepared to share in his glory.

That was the case of the biblical character Job. The devil had sought permission from God to test him. He had taken away everything that belonged to him as well as inflicting his body.

Nevertheless, he was able to worship God, claiming, "Naked I came from my mother's womb, and naked shall I return. The Lord gave, and the Lord has taken away; blessed be the name of the Lord" (Job 1:21).

Similarly, as believers, we should be able to continue to stay loyal to God and to worship him amid trials in the hope that we will eventually be rewarded if we do not give up.

Though the Lord permits believers to suffer, he will not allow anything which will overpower us. Therefore, in our time of suffering, let us continue to unwaveringly hold on to the faith, knowing that it is only preparing us for better things. Furthermore, we should always hold on to the hope that the Lord will eventually rescue us if we do not give up.

Suffering Part of the Believer's Calling

Truth be told, the secular world hates the things of God. Hence, believers may suffer simply because they do not imbibe the things of the world. If a believer separates themselves from things seen as ideal by the world, they will be condemned and criticized.

However, such criticisms should never break the believer knowing that we are not to conform to the world and its dictates. Given this, we should recognize that insofar as we are within the will of God, we should hold on to what we have.

Remember, Christ told his followers to bear their cross and follow him. Let us take a cue from the first-century believers who were dragged before the authorities, maligned, and humiliated in all forms yet held on to their faith.

They held on because they knew their reward in the Lord was certain. We also ought to hold a similar view and persist in our trials, knowing that eventually, the Lord will reward us.

To Keep the Believer Humble

When a parent disciplines their children for a wrong committed, it helps them to fall in line. Similarly, when a believer is afflicted, it helps them to obey the statutes of God.

Ordinarily, because we are human, we would like to do things our way. For that reason, trials and tribulations bring us to the realization of who we are in our relationship with God.

Secondly, trials sometimes act as a check on the believer becoming conceited because of revelations of God made known to them. That was the case with Paul when God allowed a messenger of Satan to harass him.

Suffering, for the Christian, in this world, is a tool that prepares him or her for the glory of the heavenly dwelling. Likewise, it produces steadfastness and reliance on God, knowing that he will always be present in times of our trials.

When we suffer, we should not lose heart, knowing that it might be in the will of God for our edification and sanctification.

Help the Believer Gain the Spirit of Empathy

When a believer is afflicted, it is for the comfort and salvation of their fellow believers. Their suffering helps them gain the experience to deal with any future challenges as well as help others face their challenges.

When a believer suffers because of the gospel of Christ, they gain the resilience and comfort that Christ gives to people who follow him.

Suffering for the Cause of the Gospel

A believer, like any other human, can go through suffering. However, any such suffering should not be on account of any bad activities but should be the result of doing the will of God.

We can suffer for the sake of following Christ, but the Lord has promised us salvation if we endure to the end. Certainly, we are not only heirs of God but are also fellow heirs of Christ.

Therefore, just as Christ suffered in his body and became glorified, we shall likewise be glorified, provided we suffer with him. The first-century believers suffered greatly for the cause of Christ and the Gospel.

Similarly, as believers, we ought to rejoice in our sufferings because we will be partaking in Christ's afflictions for the church.

The Mitigating Work of Christ

Christ made the ultimate sacrifice for humanity in suffering on the cross to become our Savior. Not only was he despised and rejected by men, but he was also smitten and afflicted by God.

Being God, he partook in things exclusive to humans so that through his death, he might destroy the devil who held sway over death. In this mission, he was given the cup of bitter grief by the Father, and he took it willingly, deeming it a necessary cost to pay to bring many sons to glory.

In his assumed role, he suffered and was tempted just like humans. He thus became the high priest who can empathize with humanity in our frailty.

God Never Abandons Believers to Suffer Alone

Suffering may come in different forms. They could be physical, emotional, or intellectual. It could be sickness, which may ravage the body, or persecution, which may restrict the believer's movement. Nevertheless, in such challenging times, the believer who endures grows in faith and stature.

Whatever results from suffering, the Lord always strengthens believers and refreshes them after they suffer misery. As the Psalmist wrote: "For you will not abandon my soul to Sheol or let your holy one sees corruption (Psalm 16:10)."

God's support is always abundantly present for believers so that they do not become overwhelmed by their adverse circumstances. This perspective allows them to cast their care on God, knowing he is ever present in their time of affliction.

What Attitude Should We Adopt When Going Through Suffering?

Often when we are going through tough times, the natural tendency is to become bitter and turn inwards. Sometimes if we think others are responsible for our troubles, we tend to take a stand against them. Such an attitude, however, is counterproductive.

Conversely, the right attitude to take is to bless and care for our tormentors. If your suffering is the result of something bad you did, there is no need to glory in it.

However, if you are suffering because of being a Christian, you have every right to keep your head high, knowing you are on a good course. During your time of difficulties, hold on to your Christian testimony and champion the course of Christ.

The End of Suffering

At the opening of this chapter, we saw how the Psalmist questioned why evil doers seemed to do well whilst the righteous suffer. Whatever the fate of the non-believer will be, we know that those who put their trust in the Lord will suffer but only for a time.

Whilst suffering is not desirable, particularly at the time it is ongoing, in the long run, it goes to test the genuineness of the believer's faith. It eventually strengthens the believer as gold is strengthened when it is refined through fire.

When a believer suffers, he or she is sharing Christ's experience so that they might also share in his abundant comfort. The good news is that suffering is only temporary; on Christ's return, he will crush Satan, the orchestrator of the believer's suffering, under his feet.

Moreover, he will wipe away our tears because death, mourning, and any painful experience will be swept away.

CHAPTER 9

Away from Me, Satan

*"And he said to them, 'I saw Satan fall
like lightning from heaven'"*
Luke 10:18

The Fall of Satan

Many people are afraid of the devil and demons. This fear may or may not be genuine. No matter how one feels about the subject, one must study it closely so that they are not assailed by the devil, Satan, and his demons.

Satan is the name normally used to describe God's fallen angel Lucifer. He was the epitome of perfection both in stature and in his standing among the angels of God. At the height of his glory, he was full of wisdom and was the embodiment of beauty.

In his splendor, he was adorned with every precious stone one could think about. This beautiful creature was blameless in his ways and ministered to God at the head of all the angels. He was indeed a guardian cherub who walked among the fiery stones and functioned as a shield for the throne of God.

At a point in his ministry, he became prideful and sought self-adulation. This stance led him to rise against God who hitherto had been his object of worship.

In Luke's Gospel chapter 10 and verse 18, Jesus made this observation; "I saw Satan fall like lightning from heaven." Jesus' pronouncement unveiled the struggle that ensued between Lucifer and the angels of God in Eden.

At the same time, it foretold of the fight in heaven between Michael and his angels on one side, and Lucifer and his angels on the other. In the said battle, the devil and his angels suffered defeat and were thrown out of heaven.

Thus, Lucifer lost his place and position in heaven and became a tormentor of the inhabitants of the earth. Satan is a tormentor whose sole aim is to deceive and bully believers and nonbelievers alike and to get them to bow to his will.

Satan as the Accuser and the Tempter

It is a fact that Satan has fallen, and he certainly does not want to take the drop alone. He desires to take others with him. For that reason, he does everything within his power to trap others.

That was what he did with Eve, craftily misleading her into believing God was the one who was deceiving them. The devil's deceptive acts did not end with Eve. He still tries at any time, and everywhere he gets the chance.

He can take things up with an individual alone or even in the presence of God. He plays his sham acts on people, always taking opportunities with both hands. That was the ploy he used with Eve. He made sure Adam was not with her before he approached.

Likewise in the presence of God, he acknowledges the believer's faithfulness but asks God to take away certain privileges so that they will not have any incentive to continue to faithfully follow him.

He did that to Job and continued to do that to countless men and women of God throughout the ages.

The devil is not just deceptive but also daring. He dared to even tempt our Lord Jesus. Remember the occasion when the Spirit led Jesus into the wilderness. Here, after Jesus had fasted for a long period, the devil came at him.

His first temptation was that of ego. He dared Jesus to turn stones into bread if he was the son of God. The second was a temptation of trust. The devil wanted to dare Jesus to find out if he could repose his trust in God. The last was that of authority. He wanted to know how badly Jesus wanted authority on earth.

These three things, a desire for recognition, a desire for power, and a desire to see if God is faithful to his word, often land men and women of God in trouble.

We should never lose sight of who God is and what he can do on our behalf. Again, we should never fail to recognize that as God's servants, all he needs from us is obedience.

When we make the pursuit of fame, and vainglory our main purpose in life, we open ourselves to the devil to not only tempt us but to accuse us unnecessarily before our God and king. It was this same desire for power and financial gain that led Judas Iscariot to betray Jesus.

When we are zealous for the things of God, we become perfect candidates for the devil to try to accuse us and enlist us in his cause. Remember, how when Peter determined to stand for Jesus as he goes the way of the cross, Satan demanded to have him on his side? Except for the intervention of the Lord Jesus, Peter would not have become the person we know now: the leader of the flock of God.

For these reasons, let us be humble but also watchful so that we do not fall prey to the evil machinations of the devil. Let us bear in mind that though Satan is the accuser and tempter, sometimes, as believers, we open ourselves to his schemes. We are unable to control our desires and therefore, he steps in.

The Works of Satan

Satan works in various ways to attract people to follow his errant path. He works in different capacities and under different circumstances. Therefore, we need to pay attention to his tricks and intrigues so that we do not become his fallen guys.

Satan puts Impediments in the Believer's Way

Satan puts obstacles in the path of believers by either hindering them or deceiving them into saying or doing things they know too well they should not say or do.

In his letter to the Thessalonian Christians, the apostle Paul intimated that he desired to visit them on different occasions, but Satan hindered him. Just as he prevented Paul from visiting and encouraging his followers, he put obstacles in our ways, in our marriages, at work, and in our lives generally.

Many times, the devil tempts believers to practice and assume deceptive ways. He did this to Ananias and Sapphira to resort to deception to deceive the apostles as regards their giving to the needs of the church.

This couple fell to their destruction because they desired vainglory. They could not speak the truth because the devil had prompted them to hold on to their possessions instead of truly letting go and allowing God to control their lives.

The Devil can Take People's Mind from God and His Word

Every believer should be aware that the devil labors around the clock to take captives. He works particularly among unbelievers, 'the sons of disobedience,' and tries to outwit believers who let down their guard.

We can see this even among the twelve the Lord himself chose, in the person of Judas Iscariot, who betrayed him. Judas fell to the devil's schemes and maneuverings because of greed and his way of thinking.

Similarly, as believers, we ought to be attentive to the still, small voice within us so that we will not be tricked into doing the bidding of the devil. At the onset of an undertaking, if your conscience does not trouble you, then you are on the right course.

You know, sometimes the devil works against people so that we fail to pay attention to the subconscious inklings and hunches. He skews our understanding so that we are not able to hear the still, small voice prompting and alerting us.

Moreover, he works hard to divert our attention from the things of God and particularly to understand the Gospel message.

Satan can Inhabit the Lives of People

Satan can inhabit the lives of people either for a brief time or a protracted period. The life of Peter exemplified the former. One day after Jesus enquired from his disciples what people thought of him, Peter rightfully said he was 'the Christ, the son of the living God.' This led to the adulation of Peter by his master.

That praise, however, was short-lived. Shortly after, he rebuked Jesus for speaking about his crucifixion. This led Jesus to condemn the devil, who he recognized had inspired the disciple's misplaced denial of the impending event.

The second instance it took over the life of a human for a protracted time is seen in the life of a woman who had been crippled by a spirit for eighteen years. In this instance, as Luke recounted, Jesus called out to her and healed her.

The way Satan can influence even the staunchest of Christians is to disguise himself as an angel of light. In that form, he can deceptively entice any unwary Christian.

Characteristics of the Sinful Person and why they Cannot Stand the Evil One

The sinful person is deceitful, wicked, and hates everything righteous. Perhaps the greatest liability is shunning the truth in their lives, always bending it to suit their whims and caprice.

They not only sin all the time, but they make it a habit. Oftentimes they will boast about their wicked activities to their friends and foes alike. The devil, who is the god of this world, has blinded their minds and keeps them from seeing the light that the gospel of Christ brings.

They seldom or never do what is right in the eyes of God. Neither do they give God pride of place in their lives. Above all, they have a distorted image of God and often blaspheme his name without any reservation.

Since sinful individuals exhibit these characteristics, they cannot resist the devil because they have nothing with which to fight.

Characteristics of the Righteous Person and their Weapons for Overcoming the Evil One

The contrast to the life of the sinful person is that of the righteous. Such a person is upright in all his ways and is constantly in tune with God. His actions are dictated by his desire to please God.

Such people do not make a practice of sinning because they recognize it as lawlessness. For them, anything that goes against the law of God is mayhem. They are circumspect in their actions recognizing that Christ Jesus came to take away the sins of the world.

Since the righteous do not make a habit of sinning, they do not give any opportunities to the devil to cause trouble. Moreover, their uprightness ensures them God's protection, so the devil is unable to touch them.

Ways to Overcome the Devil

There are practical and feasible ways for the believer to overcome the devil. First, they ought to recognize their position in the Lord so that they will realize the authority they possess over the devil. Jesus said, "the ruler of this world is coming, [but] he has no claim on me."

What he implied was that, because there was no sin in his life, the devil had no means to accuse him. Similarly, if believers keep away from sin, and submit to God, they will be able to resist the devil. Our lives, lived right, become a powerful testimony that defeats the devil.

Likewise, we ought to recognize that the weapons available to us in our war with the devil have divine power to destroy strongholds. Thus, we do not fight in the flesh, but we always make our supplications known to the Lord, who is the captain of the host.

Moreover, we prevail when we put on the full armor of God which is derived from knowing and using his word to aid us in prayer.

Blocking the Channels of Temptation

In normal warfare, the first line of attack is always defense. This can be applied in the spiritual realm, where believers hold their own against the devil. We can apply this strategy by living upright lives.

As a believer, if you constantly remain on your toes, you will always block any channels of temptation that could lead to entrapment. This includes watching our thought patterns and guarding our actions. This was what Eve failed to do, which allowed the devil to play mind games with her to disobey God's directives.

The Fate of the Devil and his Agents

The death of Jesus on the cross plays a vital role in the fate of the devil and his agents. Through his death, he destroyed the devil and loosened his grip over death. Jesus' stranglehold over the devil will be complete upon his return. On that day, he will crush Satan under the feet of the believer.

The fate of the unbeliever, though, will be different. On the Day of Judgment, God will tell them, "Depart from me, you cursed, into the eternal fire prepared for the devil and his angels" (Matthew 25:41).

These people include those who never gave their lives to Christ, as well as people who attended church often but never really left the camp of the devil.

God a Canopy for Believers from Satan's Fiery Darts

There is no gainsaying the fact that the believer always faces the fiery dart of the devil. However, God is a fortress that provides refuge to the believer. God's provision extends protection from the fowler's snare, deadly pestilence, and fiery darts of the devil.

Thus, he is the believer's canopy shielding him from the terror of time or the unseen arrows that fly in the dark. God offers abundant life to all who believe in him, and he keeps them from the devil.

God protects the true believer, and he is inseparable from him. Accordingly, notwithstanding the believers standing in the society or their ability, God will still be with him or her because he has said in his word that "nothing shall be able to separate us from him."

CHAPTER 10

Will I Live Again?

"The dead do not praise the Lord, nor do any who go down into silence."
Psalm 115:17

Where do the Dead go to?

Kofi Mensah beamed with a smile as he headed home from school. He was happy because he had just received a favorable reply from the college he had applied to. However, as he entered the two-bedroom apartment he shared with his parents, that smile faded from his face.

Upon entering the house, he saw his mother surrounded by several women in mourning clothes. "What could be going on," he thought.

Seeing the confusion on his face, one woman calmly broke the news to him. His father had just passed away. He broke down and started crying uncontrollably. The women tried to assure him that he would meet again with his dad in heaven.

This assurance got him more confused. "Do the dead have a place they go?" He thought. Like Kofi, most of us may be confused about our state in the afterlife. Do we have a place we will go?

Surely, humans have a destination, don't they? Is it possible that when we die, another life awaits? Is it not delusional to think that when a person dies and is buried, they would still have another life? These are more questions than we can answer, so let us take a journey into what the Bible teaches about the afterlife.

Job once posed this question; "If a man dies, shall he live again?" (Job 14:14). It is a question every generation of humanity has asked in one form or another. Scripture seeks to answer that question variously. It claims that at death, a human's breath departs from him to return to the earth.

Likewise, it asserts that the dead have no remembrance neither can that person contribute to life on earth. Moreover, it states that, unlike the living, who know what they are about, the dead know nothing.

Besides, all their emotions, be it love or hate, are no longer effectual. We can further glean meaning into the state of the dead in Job's answer to his rhetorical questions:

> For I know that my Redeemer lives, and at the last, he will stand upon the earth. And after my skin has been thus destroyed, yet in my flesh I shall see God, whom I shall see for myself, and my eyes shall behold, and not another. My heart faints within me! (Job 19:25-27)

So, Job assumed that if he lived a righteous life, he would see God upon his death. He knew that the righteous dead maintained an unbroken and constant relationship with God whether they were dead or alive. Job's belief, no doubt is the mainstream of believers. We do recognize the fact that death is not the end of existence.

The Place for the Immediate Dead

Whether or not one holds the belief, it is expedient to probe further into what exactly is taught by Scripture about the afterlife.

The clearest teaching about the afterlife is contained in the teaching of Jesus in the parable of "the Rich Man and Lazarus," in Luke 6:19-31. In this parable, Jesus showed that there are two main places the dead go soon after leaving their earthly bodies. These are Abraham's side (16:22) and 'Hades' (16:23).

Abraham's side is depicted as a place of bliss, whilst Hades is depicted as a place of torment. In between the two compartments is "a great chasm" which prevents any type of movement between them. Another name for Abraham's side is 'Paradise' (Luke 23: 43), where Jesus promised to take the thief who was crucified alongside him.

Additionally, the Bible gives further evidence that the body, which it refers to as dust, returns to its place of origin, the earth, whilst the spirit returns to its originator, God. This happens so that it would not appear that God abandoned the soul of the redeemed person to Sheol, or hades, or hell nor allowed his holy one to see decay.

Death through Adam

The book of Genesis shows that God created humanity and gave him life. The unfolding drama is that the male, Adam, and thus, by derivation, the female, was formed from the dust of the ground and given the gift of life through the breath of God.

God gave humans a specific purpose to fulfill. Our first obligation was to procreate. The second was to tend to and eat from the soil.

Unfortunately, the first couple failed the test and thus forfeited the privileges they were privy to. The fall thus limited us as humans in scope and also saddled us with the burden of hard labor. The result of the fall is death, just as all other creatures created by God.

Life through Christ

The sinfulness of humanity meant that only a person who was in human flesh could make atonement. In the Garden of Eden, God had promised a SEED of the woman to crush the head of the serpent. Notice that God did not refer to seeds but SEED.

This had specific reference to a particular individual. This individual was Jesus, who was born of the Virgin Mary. Thus, in Jesus, God fulfilled that promise of the SEED.

The actualization of that promise was a sign of God's love for humanity. What Christ did by dying on the cross, was to take on his body the sins of the human race. So, in removing sin and death out of the way, Christ made it possible for human beings to receive life again.

The Resurrection of the Dead

The resurrection of the dead is a certainty. It is made possible by the death and resurrection of Jesus. In Luke 20:37-38 Jesus cited the burning bush as a reason for the reality of the resurrection. He claimed that Moses, at the sight of the burning bush, called God, the God of Abraham, Isaac, and Jacob, signifying that God is the God of the living.

Again, in his encounter with Lazarus's grieving sisters, Jesus pointed out that he is the resurrection, and that if anyone believed in him, that person would have life after his or her death. The Lord claimed that there was an approaching time when all the dead would hear his voice and come out of their tombs.

This is the time when the dead will face the consequences of their actions during their lifetime on earth and have their fates decided. The question which is often on the lips of people is: how will this happen?

Fortunately for today's believers, the first-century followers also asked the same questions. They wondered how the dead would be raised and with what kind of bodies.

In his answer, Paul countered that just as a seed sown perishes in the soil and then germinates in a new form, so would it be with humans. In the resurrection, he alluded, that the resurrected body would take on a new form as God determines.

The Dead in Christ will Rise to be with The Lord

The typical teaching about those who have died in Christ is in the teachings of the Apostle Paul in his letters to the Thessalonian and Corinthian churches. In this teaching, he affirmed his belief that since Jesus died and rose again, God will, in a similar way, bring with Jesus those who have 'fallen asleep' in him. So, to Paul, death was a temporary state that would transition the believer into a more permanent existence.

He taught that when Christ returns to earth from heaven, he will call out in a loud voice with the support of an archangel and the trumpet of God to all who believed in him whilst they were alive.

These, the apostle claimed, will be joined by those who are still alive. Together, they would be changed and be caught up in the clouds to meet him in the air and dwell with him forever.

The Place for the Wicked Dead

One thing that is certain for all humans is death. However, it is not the end of our existence. After we are dead, we will meet the Lord, and each of us will be judged by his standards. Both the believer and the unbeliever will be judged.

The unbeliever, referred to in scripture as the wicked, will not experience the same fate as the believer. Their fate will be eternal punishment in the lake that burns with fire and sulfur, which is also the abode of the devil, a place where weeping never stops.

The Place for the Righteous Dead

Scripture teaches that the righteous dead will share in the first resurrection. Their citizenship is in heaven, where they will be with their Savior, Jesus Christ. Not only are the righteous dead going to be in heaven, but they will be rewarded with eternal life, which God provides through the death of his son Jesus Christ.

This gift of eternal life is only available to those who diligently live to please God. Such people do not seek the pleasures of this world. Their major concern is to daily do God's will.

For people in this category, the second death will have no power over them. These souls will be priests of God and Christ, and they will reign with him for a thousand years. The righteous dead will be given a new body. From the way the Bible describes it, this body will be free from the pain associated with the earth.

Besides, just as the resurrected Christ had a body that could materialize and go through locked doors at will, the righteous dead, will similarly possess such attributes. They will not be limited by space or time.

A great distinctive characteristic of their new body is that it will be made to suit the heavenly surroundings that the righteous will find themselves.

Moreover, in the heavenly dwellings of the righteous, God will be their comfort and strength. Furthermore, sorrow and pain, as are mourning and a sense of loss will never be present because God will make those things of the past.

Notes

Chapter 1

The Origins and the Fall of Humanity
Genesis 1:26-30; Genesis 2:4-9,15-25; Psalm 139:14; Genesis 3:1-24; Genesis 4:1-2; 1 Timothy 2:14

The First Adam Vis-À-Vis the Second Adam
1 Corinthians 15:22-28, 45-49; Romans 5:12-19; Isaiah 43:27

Position of Humanity in the Created Order
Genesis 1:26; Psalm 8:3-4

The Spiritual Man
Galatians 2:20; Galatians 5:22-23; Romans 8:1-39; Colossians 3:12

The Carnal Man
Psalm 51:5; Jeremiah 17:9; John 21:17; Romans 8:3; 1 Corinthians 2:14; Ephesians 4:17-18; 1 John 3:8; Matthew 15:19

The Design of God for Humanity
Genesis 2:5; Genesis 8:21; 1Timothy 2:4; Galatians 4:4; John 1:14; 1 Thessalonians 1:1-10

Humanity and Christ

Colossians 1:16; 2 Corinthians 5:17; John 3:16; John 14:6; 1Timothy 2:5; Colossians 1:21-23; Galatians 3:16; Hebrews 4:15; Hebrews 2:14

Permissible Human Behavior

Deuteronomy 22:4; Leviticus 19:33-34; James 4:10; Hebrews 13:16; Philippians 2:3

Forbidden Human Behavior

Leviticus 18:22; Genesis 9:6; James 2:1-4; 1 Corinthians 6:18

Humanity and Divine Providence

Matthew 6:26; Joshua 3:16; Genesis 3:20-24

The Divine Law and the Death Penalty

Genesis 9:5-6; Exodus 21:12; Romans 13:1-7

Chapter 2

What is Sin?

James 4:17; Mark 7:20-23; 1 John 3:4; 1 John 5:17

Who is a Sinner?

Job 15:14; Psalm 51:5; Isaiah 64:6; Ecclesiastes 7:20; Romans 3:23-24; 1 John 1:8-10; 1 John 3:4; 1 John 2:11; Matthew 5:28; 1 John 3:8; Ephesians 2:1-3

What Causes Sin?

Genesis 3:1-24; Genesis 3:1-24; James 1:14-15; James 4:4; 2 Timothy 3:1-5; Matthew 24:12; Matthew 15:17-20

The Incentive to Sin
Jeremiah 17:9; Romans 1:28-32; Philippians 3:18-19

The Incentive of Sinlessness
Deuteronomy 30:15-16; 1 John 1:7-9; 2 Timothy 2:19; 1 Corinthians 6:19-20; Psalm 1191-176

The Consequences of Sin
Numbers 32:23; Isaiah 59:1-2; Romans 6:23; Romans 5:12; 2 Peter 2:4; Ezekiel 39:24; Revelation 21:8; Galatians 6:7; Galatians 5:19-21; John 8:34; 1 Corinthians 6:9-10; Revelation 22:15; Revelation 9:21

The Key to the Forgiveness of Sin
1 John 1:8-10; 1 John 1:9; Psalm 51:10; Proverbs 28:13; Psalm 51:1-2; John 3:16-17; 2 Corinthians 5:21; Psalm 32:5; Isaiah 1:18; Psalm 69:5; 1 John 1:6; Ephesians 1:7; Romans 5:8; Mark 3:28-29; Matthew 12:31-32

How to Overcome Sin
Genesis 4:7; Galatians 5:16; 1 Corinthians 10:13;1 Corinthians 15:57; James 4:7; 1 Peter 4:8; 1 John 3:6-10; James 1:14-15

What Happens When our Sins are Forgiven?
2 Corinthians 5:17; Romans 5:1-21; Matthew 5:48; Micah 7:18-19; 1 Peter 2:24; Psalm 103:9-13; Ezekiel 36:25-26

How Should the Forgiven Live?
Psalm 4:2-6; Jeremiah 31:34; John 5:14; John 20:19-23; Colossians 3:1-24

Chapter 3

The Plan of Salvation
Genesis 3: 14-15; Romans 5:8; Acts 13:48; 1 Thessalonians 5:9; 2 Thessalonians 2:13; 2 Corinthians 6:2

All have Sinned
Romans 3:10, 23; Isaiah 64:6

Salvation is by Grace
Ephesians 2:1-22;S Titus 2:11; Romans 3:20; Acts 15:7-15; Galatians 2:21; Romans 6:14; Romans 6:1-2

Salvation was Initiated by God
John 3:16; Ephesians 1:4; Philippians 1:6

The Path to Salvation
John 3:3

Repentance
Acts 2:38; Acts 3:19; James 1:21; Revelation 22:11-21
Acts 11:18; Acts 17:30; 2 Peter 3:9

Belief
Mark 16:16; Matthew 7:21; Philippians 2:12; John 3: 16-18; Acts 16:30-33; 1 Peter 1:8-9

Confession
Romans 10:9-10

Acceptance
Hebrews 2:3; Matthew 7:13-14

Salvation is Only Through Jesus

John 14:6; John 15:1-27; John 10:9; Acts 4:12; Acts 2:36-41;
1 Corinthians 15:1-58; Acts 16:31; John 3:36; John 10:28; John 6:37;
1 Peter 2:24; John 11:25-26; Revelation 3:20

The State of the New Believer

John 1:12; John 5:24; Romans 6:23; 2 Corinthians 5:17
Ephesians 1:13; Romans 10:13; Galatians 3:27; Romans 8:38-39

Purpose of Salvation

John 3:16-17; 1 John 5:13; Revelation 3:5; Acts 2:41;
Romans 8:37-39; Titus 3:5; 2 Corinthians 5:21; 2 Timothy 1:9

The Believer's Responsibility in God's Plan of Salvation

Hebrews 6:4-6; 1 John 2:23-29; Romans 1:16; 1 Corinthians 1:21;
Mark 16:15-16; 1 Timothy 4:16; Matthew 7:21-23; Ephesians 2:10

Chapter 4

Can one Fall from Grace?

Hebrews 6:4-6; Hebrews 10:26-29; Philippians 2:12

Salvation is a Gift from God

John 3:16, 36; John 20:31; Ephesians 2:8-10; Romans 6:23; Romans
11:29; Romans 11:6; Psalm 34:22

The Believer is Sealed by the Holy Spirit

Romans 5:1-21; 2 Corinthians 5:17-18; Romans 3:24; Romans 5:18;
Romans 8:1-39; Ephesians 2:19; Hebrews 10:36

The Believer Becomes an Inseparable Child of God
Ecclesiastes 3:14; John 1:12; John 3:18; Romans 8:38-39; 1 John 5:10-13; 1 Peter 1:1-25; Ephesians 1:1-23; 1 Thessalonians 5:23-24

The Believer can no Longer Live in Sin
1 John 4:4; 1 John 3:6; 1 John 3:6-9; 1 John 3:18-21; Galatians 5:4; Galatians 6:8-9; Hebrews 5:11-14; Hebrews 7:25; John 6:50-71

God Guaranteed the Eternal Security of the Believer
Colossians 2:13-14; Titus 1:1-2; Luke 15:3-7; 1 Corinthians 1:6-9; Psalm 119:165; John 17:2; Colossians 1:13

Jesus Guaranteed the Eternal Security of the Believer
John 4:14; John 10:27-29; John 6:37; John 5:24; John 6:47; 1 John 5:13; 2 Peter 3:9; Ephesians 1:11; Jude 1:21, 24; Hebrews 9:15

The Believer is Sealed by the Holy Spirit
Acts 2:38-39; Ephesians 4:30; Ephesians 1:13-14; 2 Corinthians 5:1-5; 2 Corinthians 1:22; Romans 8:9

Jesus' Sacrifice was Final
Hebrews 10:14; Hebrews 9:12; John 6:40; 1 Peter 3:18-22; Hebrews 5:9

Those Truly Saved will Remain in the Lord
Luke 8:13; 1 John 2:19; 1 Peter 1:4-5; Philippians 3:20-21; 1 Peter 1:23

Salvation as a Life-Long Process
Romans 8:28-31; Philippians 1:6; 1 Thessalonians 3:12-13; 2 Timothy 4:18

The Believer Should Mature in Faith
Galatians 4:1-5:26; John 15:15

Christ Can Hold on to His Saints
Jude 1:24-25; 2 Timothy 2:19; John 6:39

Chapter 5

God the Initiator of Redemption
1 Kings 1:29; Isaiah 43:1-2; Job 19:25-27; Ephesians 1:1-23; Isaiah 44:21-22; Revelation 5:10; Colossians 1:13-14

The Role of Blood in Redemption
Ephesians 1:7; 1 Peter 1:18-19; Revelation 5:9; Leviticus 17:11

The Difference in Blood of Animals and Christ
Hebrews 9:12; Galatians 2:20; 1 Peter 1:19; Colossians 1:14; Colossians 1:20-22; Romans 3:23-25

Israel's Redemptive Practices Forefront Human Redemption
Leviticus 25:25-34; Numbers 3:46-51; Ruth 3:6-18; Ruth 4:3-10

The Redemptive Work of Christ
Colossians 1:15-17;Titus 2:14; Romans 3:25; Matthew 20:28;1 John 3:16; 1 Corinthians 1:30; Hebrews 9:15; 2 Corinthians 5:1-21; Isaiah 53:1-12

Christ's Work Offered Justification
Romans 3:24-26; Romans 5:18; John 3:16-17; Revelation 5:9-10

Christ's Work Offered Redemption from the Hold of the Law
Galatians 3:13; Galatians 4:4-5; 1 Corinthians 7:23; Psalm 111:9; Romans 6:4

The Human Role in Redemption
Romans 10:9-10; 2 Peter 3:9; Luke 21:25-28; 1 Corinthians 6:20

The Lifestyle Befitting the Redeemed
Ephesians 4:1-32; Ephesians 5:1-33; Acts 20:28; Romans 2:4

Redemption Should Lead to Christlikeness
1 John 3:2; 1 John 3:3; Romans 5:10; Matthew 5:48; James 1:2-4; Romans 12:1-2

Chapter 6

Restitution is a U-Turn
Matthew 5:23-24; Numbers 5:5-7

Restitution is Accountability
Genesis 9:5-6; Leviticus 5:15; Exodus 22:7; Galatians 6:1

Restitution is a Sign of Genuine Repentance
Luke 19:1-10

Restitution is to Ensure Fairness
Nehemiah 5; Exodus 21

Restitution is to Build a Fraternity of Believers
Romans 13:8-10; Numbers 5:6-7; Leviticus 6:1-7; Judges 17:1-3

Return, and then Some
Exodus 22:1-16; Leviticus 6:2-5

God Reinstates the Repentant
2 Corinthians 5:21; Joel 2:25; Amos 9:14; Ezekiel 33:14-16

Chapter 7

God, the Architect of Reconciliation
Isaiah 25:6-8; John 3:16-17; Ephesians 1:3-10; 2 Corinthians 5:17-21; Luke 15:11-32

Christ Made Reconciliation a Possibility
Isaiah 53:1-12; Romans 4:25; 2 Corinthians 5:14-15, 21; 1 Peter 2:24

Christ, the Channel of Reconciliation
2 Corinthians 5:19; Colossians 1:20-22; Ephesians 2:15-18; Romans 5:1-21

The Role of Blood in Reconciliation
1 John 1:7; 1 John 5:6; Leviticus 17:14; Ezekiel 16:6; Hebrews 13:12; Hebrews 9:12-14; Matthew 26:28; Revelation 1:5; Hebrews 9: 11-28; Ephesians 2: 11-22; Romans 5:6-11

Reconciliation Preferred to Sacrifice
Matthew 5:23-26; Mark 11:25; Romans 12:1-2; Hosea 6:6; John 15:12-14; Philippians 2:4; 1 Peter 2:4-10; 1 Samuel 15:22; Psalm 40:6; Philippians 2:17; Ephesians 5:1-2

Prescribed Ways to Achieve Reconciliation
Hebrews 12:14; Romans 12:1-2; Matthew 18:15-17; 2 Corinthians 2:5-11

We are Partakers of Reconciliation
Isaiah 61:1-4; Isaiah 52:7; 2 Corinthians 5:18-20; Colossians 3:13; Luke 17:3-4; Matthew 6:14-15; Ephesians 4:17-32

Divine Initiative the Standard for Reconciliation
Matthew 18:21-35; Ephesians 4:32; Luke 23:34

Reconciliation Demands Selflessness
Luke 6:27-42; Romans 12:14-21; Matthew 7:12; Philippians 2:1-13;
Ephesians 4:1-3; Genesis 33:4

Chapter 8

The Age-Old Question: Why do Good People Suffer?
Psalm 37; 1 Corinthians 13:3

The Purpose of Suffering
John 9:1-3

For Restoration
Romans 5:3-5; Philippians 3:10; 1 Peter 5:10

To Make the Believer Steadfast in Faith
Deuteronomy 8:3; Job 36:15; Jeremiah 29:11; Acts 9:16; Acts
14:22; Romans 8:29, 35-39; 2 Corinthians 4:16-18; 2 Timothy 2:3;
James 5:10-11; Hebrews 12:11; 1 Peter 4:1; Revelation 2:10

As a Test of Faith
Job 1:20-21; 1 Peter 4:12-19; James 1:2, 12; 2 Corinthians 4:8-10;
2 Corinthians 4:17; 2 Corinthians 1:3-4; Romans 8:28-29; 1
Corinthians 10:13; 1 Peter 4:12-13

Suffering Part of the Believer's Calling
John 15:19; John 16:33; Luke 14:27; Matthew 10:22; Acts 5:41;
1 Peter 2:19; 1 Peter 2:21 Matthew 10:38; Romans 8:17-18; 2
Timothy 3:12; Philippians 1:29; Matthew 5:10-12; 2 Corinthians
12:10; 1 Peter 2:19-21

To Keep the Believer Humble
Psalm 119:71; 2 Corinthians 12:7-10; Romans 5:1-21; Romans 8:18; James 1:2-4; Romans 8:28

Help the Believer Gain the Spirit of Empathy
2 Corinthians 1:3-7; Galatians; 2 Corinthians 1:3-5

Suffering for the Cause of the Gospel
Mark 13:13;1 Peter 3:17; Acts 17:10-11; Romans 8:17; 1 Peter 3:14; Colossians 1:24

The Mitigating Work of Christ
Isaiah 52:13-15; Isaiah 53:3-4; John 18:11; Hebrews 2:10; Hebrews 2:14; Hebrews 4:15-16; 1 Peter 3:18; Matthew 27:28-29; Hebrews 9:26; Matthew 26:39; Hebrews 4:15; Romans 8:3; Matthew 4:24

God Never Abandons Believers to Suffer Alone
Psalm 73:26; Psalm 34:19; Psalm 119:50; Psalm 16:10; Isaiah 43:2; Psalm 22:1-31; Psalm 23:1-6; 1 Peter 5:7; Job 13:15; 1 Corinthians 2:9

What Attitude Should We Adopt When Going Through Suffering?
Romans 12:14; Matthew 10:39; 1 Peter 4:13; 1 Peter 4:16; 2 Timothy 1:8

The End of Suffering
2 Corinthians 1:5; 1 Peter 1:6-7; Romans 16:20; Revelation 21:4

Chapter 9

The Fall of Satan
Ezekiel 28:11-19; Isaiah 14:11-15; Revelation 12:7-12; Luke 10:18

Satan as the Accuser and the Tempter
Genesis 3:1; Job 1:6-12; Matthew 4:1-11; Luke 4:5-6; John 13:2; Luke 22:31-32; 1 Peter 5:8-9; James 1:13-15; 1 Corinthians 10:13; Revelation 2:10; 2 Corinthians 11:14

The Works of Satan
Satan Puts Impediments In The BELIEVER'S Way
1 Thessalonians 2:18; Act 5:3

The Devil can Take People's Mind from God and His Word
Matthew 13:19; John 6:70; 2 Corinthians 2:10-11; Ephesians 2:2

Satan can Inhabit the Lives of People
2 Corinthians 11:14; Matthew 16:23; Luke 13:10-13, 16; Matthew 4:10

Characteristics of the Sinful Person and why they Cannot Stand the Evil One
Acts 13:10; 1 John 3:4-10; 2 Corinthians 4:4; Ephesians 2:1-2

Characteristics of the Righteous Person and their Weapons for Overcoming the Evil One
Jeremiah 29:13; John 8:44; 1 John 3:4-10; 1 John 5:18-19; Ephesians 4:26-27

Ways to Overcome the Devil
John 14:30; Luke 10:19; James 4:7; 2 Corinthians 10:3-5; Ephesians 6:10-20; Revelation 12:10-11; 1 John 4:4; Jude 1:8-9

Blocking the Channels of Temptation
Isaiah 8:19; 1 Corinthians 7:5; 2 Corinthians 11:3; 2 Timothy 2:26

The Fate of the Devil and his Agents
Matthew 25:41; Romans 16:20; James 2:19; Hebrews 2:14;
Revelation 12:9; Revelation 20:2, 10; Revelation 21:8

God a Canopy for Believers from Satan's Fiery Darts
Psalm 91:1-16; John 10:10; John 17:15; Romans 8:38-39

Chapter 10

Where do the Dead go to?
Job 14:14; Psalm 146:4; Psalm 6:5; Ecclesiastes 9:5-6
Psalm 115:17; Job 19:25-27

The Place for the Immediate Dead
Luke 6: 19-31; Luke 23:43; Ecclesiastes 12:7; Psalm 16:10;
Rev. 6:9-11

Death through Adam
Genesis 2:7-9, 15-17 Genesis 3:19, 24; Ecclesiastes 3:19-20;
Romans 5:12

Life through Christ
John 3:16; 1 Peter 2:24; John 20:31; John 11:25-26; Revelation 1:18;
1 Peter 2:24; John 5:24; John 3:18; 1 Corinthians 15:54; Romans
8:13; John 14:6

The Resurrection of the Dead
John 11:25; John 5: 28-29; 1 Corinthians 15:35-54; 1 Corinthians
15:51-57; Luke 20:37-38; Thessalonians 4:14; Daniel 12:2

The Dead in Christ will Rise to be with The Lord
1 Thessalonians 4:13-18; 1 Corinthians 15:51

The Place for the Wicked Dead

Hebrews 9:27; Revelation 21:8; Revelation 14:11; Matthew 25:46; Revelation 2:11; Matthew 10:28; Matthew 25:41; Isaiah 14:9-11; Matthew 8:11-12

The Place for the Righteous Dead

Philippians 3:20; Revelation 14:13; Matthew 25:46; Revelation 2:11; Revelation 20:6; 2 Corinthians 5:1-8; Philippians 3:20-21; John 14:1-3; 2 Corinthians 5:6-8; Revelation 1:6; 1 John 5:13; 1 Corinthians 15:53; Romans 2:7; John 3:14; John 11:26; Revelation 21:4

About the Author

Pastor and teacher **Akwasi Oppong Ofori** is an ordained minister of the Ghana Baptist Convention. Formerly the Lead Pastor at Solid Rock Baptist Church in Aurora, Colorado, he also served as the first chairperson of the North American Baptist Association of the Ghana Baptist Convention. He is the author of two other books, *Recovering Storytelling for Ghanaian Preaching*, and *I Will Lift Up My Cup*. Originally trained as a teacher at the Wesley College of Education in Kumasi Ghana, he has a Diploma in Biblical Studies and a Bachelor of Theology (BTh) degrees from the Christian Service University College in Kumasi Ghana and the International Baptist Theological Seminary in Prague the Czech Republic respectively. Rev. Ofori also holds a Master of Divinity (M. Div.) from Denver Seminary in Colorado, USA, and a Master of theology (Th.M.) from the Toronto School of Theology of the University of Toronto Canada. Rev. Ofori is completed by his wife and two surviving children.